500
FANTASTIC CARS

Serge Bellu

500
FANTASTIC CARS

SOLAR

© 2002, Éditions SOLAR

Éditions SOLAR

12, avenue d'Italie

75013 Paris

France

Internet: www.solar.tm.fr

Series director: Renaud de Laborderie

Page design: Graph'M

This edition first published in 2003 by Haynes Publishing

Reprinted 2004

Translated into English by Jon Pressnell

A catalogue record for this book is available from the
British Library.

ISBN 1 84425 039 3

Library of Congress Catalog Card No. 2003110423

Haynes Publishing, Sparkford,
Yeovil, Somerset BA22 7JJ, UK
Tel: 01963 442030 Fax: 01963 440001
Int. tel: +44 1963 442030 Fax: +44 1963 440001
E-mail: sales@haynes-manuals.co.uk
Web site: www.haynes.co.uk

Haynes North America Inc., 861 Lawrence Drive,
Newbury Park, California 91320, USA

Printed in Italy

THE HISTORY OF THE FUTURE
500 DREAM CARS

Whether you call them concept cars or prototypes, dream cars or special bodies, all these cars have a dream as the reason for their existence. The terminology varies with the era and with the latitude, but whatever name you give them, these creations have always had as their aim the exploration of a future that is to a greater or lesser degree near and to a greater or lesser degree realistic. Some project themselves into a radical avant-garde, while others anticipate models that will have a commercial future. Conceived by the car manufacturers themselves or by independent design houses, these concept cars have the ambition to send out on behalf of their progenitors a message of creativity, innovation and dynamism, while venerating the religion of the future.

Concept cars are a declaration of intent, by its very nature excessive and in a certain manner doomed to obsolescence. These visions dramatise the convulsions of the present: to imagine new rules for tomorrow, concept cars exalt the tremors of their own time. Sometimes with opportunism, often with premonition, they give expression to the formidable powers of reaction possessed by a car industry faced with the desires and necessities that evolve with the rhythm of different lifestyles.

Since the dawn of the motor-car, original-minded creators have tried to project themselves into the future. Here is their history, told through their most outstanding realisations. The list is not exhaustive. Arbitrarily we have selected eight vehicles per year for the period from 1952 onwards, after offering an overview of the first half of the century. For each even year an additional car has been pulled out and given a detailed analysis. We have excluded the numerous special bodies, those models bodied by the various coachbuilders and which until the 1950s constituted the bulk of the market in luxury vehicles. We have also avoided presenting prototypes which ultimately gave birth to production vehicles. The selection, perforce subjective, concentrates on genuine research prototypes and puts the emphasis on the most innovative and the most spectacular vehicles.

AT THE DAWN OF THE CENTURY, WHEN CARS WERE FOR THE MOST PART STILL RELATED TO HORSE-DRAWN VEHICLES, THE FIRST GLIMMERINGS OF EMANCIPATION STARTED TO SHOW...

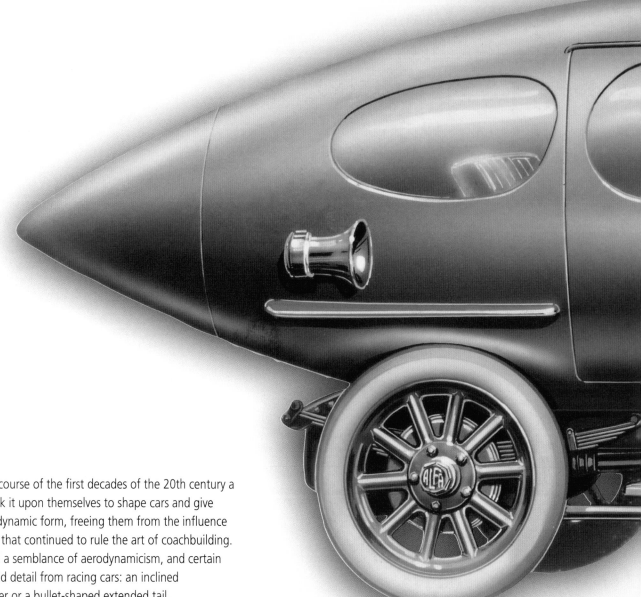

Milan, **1914**. In the course of the first decades of the 20th century a few visionaries took it upon themselves to shape cars and give them a more aerodynamic form, freeing them from the influence of the horse-drawn carriage that continued to rule the art of coachbuilding. Some bodyshops introduced a semblance of aerodynamicism, and certain closed cars borrowed the odd detail from racing cars: an inclined windscreen, a rounded corner or a bullet-shaped extended tail.

But beyond these numerous timid or plain inept efforts stood a radical and startling project: an Alfa Romeo 40-60hp clad with an all-enveloping one-volume shell, dreamt up by the Milan coachbuilder Castagna in response to an order from Count Mario Ricotti.

Seemingly an escapee from a Jules Verne novel, this extraordinary vehicle had a streamlined fuselage like that of an aircraft, pierced with large portholes. In an automotive world still populated by phaetons, berlines and landaulets inherited from the era of horse-drawn vehicles, Ricotti's Alfa Romeo stunned with its soft forms, its prow completely enclosing the engine compartment, and its tail drawn out like a torpedo.

Under this futurist body, however, the mechanicals were as archaic as ever, with the high-set side-members sitting above the axles and giving a sit-up-and-beg old-fashioned silhouette to this otherwise sci-fi machine.

In spite of the one-box form of the body, the driving position was not brought forward, because the bulky engine was of course very much present under the profiled front. The radiator, too, remained upright, but was to all intents shrouded by the curves of the aerodynamic bodyshell.

ALFA ROMEO 40-60 HP (CASTAGNA)

The 40-60hp chassis was in itself a rare item, as only 27 examples were built. The engine was made up of two separate blocks, with overhead valves – one of its few modern features; it was a four-cylinder unit of 6,082cc, developing 70bhp at 2,200rpm.

In 1915 the car was converted into an open tourer at the request of its eccentric owner. The pot-bellied lower quarters and the curved prow were nonetheless preserved.

One-box and aerodynamic, the Alfa's body was in many respects ahead of the time. Alas, this modernism of form was counterbalanced by the archaism of the mechanicals.

CLAVEAU 9 CV AUTOBLOC C.I.R.

CLAVEAU 9 CV AUTOBLOC C.I.R. **Paris, October 1927**. One year after the first Auto-bloc prototypes, which were open cars (a two-seater and a four-seater, in 1926), Emile Claveau returned with a closed model, an aerodynamic single-box design of lightweight monocoque construction, with all-round independent suspension. Engine: rear-mounted 1,498cc air-cooled flat-four. Gearbox: three speed. Wheelbase: 320cm. Weight: 1,050kg.

LEYAT HÉLICA

LEY T6 (SPOHN)

LEY T6 (SPOHN)

Friedrichshafen a.B., February 1922. Having learnt from the construction of the Zeppelin airships, Paul Jaray carried out windtunnel tests which led to the evolution of a fluid, all-enveloping form. He applied his theories to several prototypes, with the first being financed by Ley; an Audi, a Dixi and an Apollo followed. Engine: 1,540cc 4-cyl. Power: 20bhp. Wheelbase: 267cm.

NORTH-LUCAS

NORTH-LUCAS **London, November 1922**. Prototype conceived by the engineer Oliver D North, and sponsored by financier Ralph Lucas. The car was built by the Robin Hood Engineering Works Ltd, with coachwork by the Chelsea Motor Building Co Ltd. The rear-mounted engine was a 5-cylinder air-cooled radial of 1.5 litres, and there was four-wheel independent suspension.

LEYAT HÉLICA **Paris, June 1921**. The free-thinking Marcel Leyat pro-duced prop-driven cars from 1912 to 1925. The Hélica took the form of a tapering fuselage made of stretched and doped fabric, aircraft-style, and powered by a propeller positioned to form the car's prow; the driver piloted this unstable contraption – with rear-wheel steering! – by look-ing through the propeller. Engine: 1,203cc flat-twin. Wheelbase: 295cm.

PERSU AUTOMOBIL AERODYNAMIC

PERSU AUTOMOBIL AERODYNAMIC **Berlin, November 1923**. The Romanian engineer Aurel Persu came up with this aerodynamic prototype with a two-box body: a very cab-forward passenger compartment, tapering towards the rear, and an engine compartment in the centre. The all-enveloping body covered the wheels. The four-cylinder engine (1.4-litre and 22bhp) was made in Berlin by the AGA-Werke.

HISPANO-SUIZA H6C (NIEUPORT)

HISPANO-SUIZA H6C (NIEUPORT) **Palermo, April 1924**. Competition car built to the order of André Dubonnet to contest the 1924 Targa Florio. The body, in tulip wood, was constructed on chassis 10743 by aeronautical firm Nieuport-Astra. Engine: 7,953cc straight-six.

BENZ RH **Mannheim, July 1924**. After having built three Type RH racing cars for the 1922 Italian GP, Benz developed a 'civilian' version with headlamps and wings, for road use. The car's configuration, with a mid-mounted engine, was inspired by the work of Edmund Rumpler. Engine: 1,997cc 6-cyl. Power: 80bhp. Wheelbase: 277.9cm.

BENZ RH

FARMAN A6B SPORT **Boulogne-Billancourt, March 1923**. Streamlined closed car with shrouded chassis members and smooth-lined fuselage flanked by long flat wings, characterised by its ultra-flat passenger compartment and the integration of the twin spare wheels in the pointed rear. Engine: 6,597cc. Power: 165bhp. Wheelbase: 360cm.

FARMAN A6B SPORT

AUBURN CABIN SPEEDSTER

CLAVEAU 6 CV CONDUITE INTÉRIEURE

AUBURN CABIN SPEEDSTER **New York, January 1929.** Streamlined coupé based on the eight-cylinder Auburn 8-120; designed by Alan Leamy and aviator Wade Morton. Aluminium body by Griswold of Detroit. Exhibited at the Los Angeles Auto Show, after its New York debut, the car was destroyed in March in the fire that ravaged the Californian show. Wheelbase: 304.8cm.

BURNEY STREAMLINER (CARLTON)

BURNEY STREAMLINER (CARLTON) **London, 1929.** Rear-engined aerodynamic prototype using fwd Alvis 12/75 mechanicals turned back-to-front. The car was the work of Streamline Cars Ltd, founded by Charles Dennistoun Burney. Crossley acquired the licence to build the Burney, and displayed the car at the 1933 London motor show – resulting in a paltry 24 sales.

OPEL RAK 2 **Geneva, March 1929.** More than a simple record-breaker, the 'Rocket Car' was a real attention-grabber on Opel's stand at the Geneva motor show. On 23 May 1928, in the hands of Kurt Volhart, it had hit 143mph at Berlin's Avus track, thanks to the twelve rockets that powered it.

SENSAUD DE LAVAUD 17 HP

SENSAUD DE LAVAUD 17 HP **Paris, October 1927.** In 1927 and 1928 Robert Dimitri Sensaud de Lavaud showed some interesting prototypes at the Paris salon – in both bare-chassis and closed coupé forms. The chassis was of cast aluminium, and the front suspension was independent, articulating around a large central pivot, while the six-cylinder 2,650cc engine was mated to an experimental automatic transmission. Wheelbase: 320cm.

OPEL RAK 2

CLAVEAU 6 CV CONDUITE INTÉRIEURE **Paris, October 1930.** Always swimming against the tide, in 1930 Emile Claveau came up with a new prototype, this time with front-wheel drive, integral construction, and pontoon bodywork. In its shape the car was inspired by the Chenard & Walcker 1500 Sport built by SPCA in 1927. Engine: 740cc 2-cyl. Power: 30bhp at 3,000rpm. Wheelbase: 240cm.

BENTLEY SPEED SIX (GURNEY NUTTING)

BENTLEY SPEED SIX (GURNEY NUTTING) **London, May 1930.** This streamlined Speed Six coupé, on chassis GJ 3811, was specially built for racing driver Woolf Barnato, Le Mans winner in 1928, 1929 and 1930. The car became famous for beating the Blue Train between Monte Carlo and Calais.

BUCCIALI DOUBLE-HUIT **Paris, October 1930.** Centre of interest at the Paris show, with its André Granet décor, this chassis heralded a splendid front-wheel-drive independent-suspension monster, powered by a 16-cylinder engine of staggered in-line configuration. This sleeve-valve engine (8,036cc and a claimed 170bhp at 3,000rpm) was shown as a mock-up. The bare chassis has been preserved in the United States.

BUCCIALI DOUBLE-HUIT

ADLER STANDARD 6 BERLINE (NEUSS)

Paris, October 1930. The architect Walter Gropius, founder of the Bauhaus, designed a range of stripped-down and functional bodies for Adler: a saloon on the Standard 6 chassis, built by Neuss (displayed at the Paris show), three Karmann-built cabriolets on the same chassis, and two limousines by Neuss on the Standard 8 chassis.

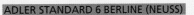

ADLER STANDARD 6 BERLINE (NEUSS)

THE WORK OF AN AVIATION PIONEER, PIERRE DELCOURT, THIS STRANGE PROTOTYPE WAS A FURTHER BRIDGE BETWEEN THE AUTOMOTIVE AND THE AERONAUTICAL.

CITROËN VENT DEBOUT (DELCOURT)

The 'Vent Debout' prototype of Pierre Delcourt was one of the stars of the Concours d'Elégance et de Confort de l'Auto in the Parc des Princes, in June 1930.

Paris, June 1930. Pierre Delcourt counts among those inventors who are as unknown as they were original. He was based in the heart of the Champagne region, in the quiet village of Vertus, of which he was mayor from 1949 until 1953. Born on 8 July 1898, Pierre Delcourt belonged to that extended family of aero-industry pioneers. He worked at Spad, in Paris, from 1916, but following the example of countless early aviators – such as Voisin, Weymann, Farman, Rumpler, Jaray and Béchereau – he turned towards the motor car in the aftermath of the First World War.

His aeronautical experience had familiarised Pierre Delcourt with the science of aerodynamics. On the base of a Citroën AC4 he therefore built a streamlined saloon distinguished by its domed roof, spatted rear wheels, flat sides, forward-raked windscreen, and lack of running boards. Despite this, the front was unaltered, and kept the vertical radiator and the bonnet of the humble Citroën. Other than its aerodynamic form, the body incorporated countless innovations, such as directional headlamps and unusual door openings.

The construction also drew on the aviation world: it was built on a wooden framework reinforced with a metal trellis, and while the lower part of the shell was panelled in steel, papier mâché was used for the upper body.

In November 1928 the mock-up was tested in the windtunnel of the Institut Aérotechnique at Saint-Cyr. The prototype was shown in Paris, on the Avenue de la Grande Armée, in May 1930. The following month, in the period 4–6 June, the car participated in the 9th Concours d'Elégance et de Confort Auto in the Parc des Princes. Cleverly christened 'Vent Debout' ('Headwind'), the prototype retained standard mechanicals, with the four-cylinder engine (1,628cc and 30bhp) sitting on a chassis of 285cm wheelbase.

After having shown this avant-garde exercise, Pierre Delcourt, disappointed by the hesitant or merely amused reaction of the public, retreated into the world of architecture.

PEERLESS XD

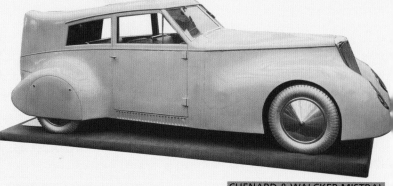

CHENARD & WALCKER MISTRAL

MAYBACH ZEPPELIN DS8 (SPOHN)

DUBONNET XÉNIA

PEERLESS XD

Cleveland, August 1931. This large saloon was the final Peerless prototype. The body, in aluminium, was designed by Frank Hershey and built by Walter Murphy of Pasadena. The sole car built is preserved in the Crayford Auto-Aviation Museum in Cleveland. Engine: 45-deg 7,603cc V16. Power: 170bhp at 3,300rpm. Wheelbase: 368.3cm.

DUBONNET XÉNIA

Paris, October 1932. Four-door saloon developed with ex-Brasier engineer Gustave Chedru. Underslung chassis with four-wheel independent suspension: each suspension unit comprised three coil springs enclosed in an oil bath. The engine was an H6C Hispano-Suiza.

CHENARD & WALCKER MISTRAL
Paris, October 1933. Two-door aerodynamic saloon on a Chenard & Walcker Aigle 8 chassis. Creator Pierre Mauboussin (1900–1984) was a graduate of the Ecole des Hautes Etudes Commerciales before adopting the two contrasting professions of jeweller and aircraft manufacturer.

VOLVO VENUS BILO (NORDBERGS)
Göteborg, November 1933. Aerodynamic saloon created to Volvo's orders by Gustaf LM Ericsson. Built on a PV653 chassis, it was characterised by its pontoon body incorporating the wings. Rather than this radical prototype, Volvo preferred the series production of a less extreme copy of the Chrysler Airflow, under the Carioca name.

VOLVO VENUS BILO (NORDBERGS)

DYMAXION CAR
New York, January 1933. Three-wheel teardrop one-box vehicle with the driving position forward of the axle line and a mid-mounted engine. First shown in New York before becoming one of the stars of the 'A Century of Progress' exhibition in Chicago. The body was designed by Starling Burgess, a naval architect, to a concept by architect Richard Buckmaster Fuller of the Dymaxion Corporation.

DYMAXION CAR

MAYBACH ZEPPELIN DS8 (SPOHN)
Paris, October 1932. Aerodynamic saloon distinguished by its pontoon lines with the wings integrated in the body sides; the coachwork was by Spohn. Engine: 6,962cc V12. Power: 150bhp at 2,800rpm. Wheelbase: 366cm.

PIERCE ARROW SILVER ARROW
New York, January 1933. Superb saloon intended to revive Pierce Arrow. The style, with its distinctive integral front wings and streamlined headlamp housings, was the work of Phil Wright. Five prototypes were built, with the first unveiled at the New York Auto Show before participating in Chicago's 'A Century of Progress' exhibition. Engine: 7,567cc V12. Power: 175bhp. Wheelbase: 353cm.

PIERCE ARROW SILVER ARROW

BRIGGS DREAM CAR (BRIGGS)
Detroit, October 1933. Unveiled at the Exhibition of Progress organised in Detroit by Ford, this rear-engined prototype was another car subsequently shown at 'A Century of Progress'. The design was by John Tjaarda, and the car was built by Briggs Manufacturing. It inspired the Lincoln Zephyr launched in November 1935.

BRIGGS DREAM CAR (BRIGGS)

BUGATTI 57 GRAND RAID

VOISIN 'VOITURE DE L'AVENIR'

BUGATTI 57 GRAND RAID Paris, October 1934.
Two-seater Type 57 roadster designed by Jean Bugatti and featuring two streamlined headrest cowlings; it was not a catalogued Bugatti model. Engine: 3,257cc 8-cyl. Power: 130bhp at 4,500rpm. Wheelbase: 330cm.

BUGATTI 57 S ROADSTER Paris, October 1936. One-off roadster with spatted wheels, the all-enclosing front wings pivoting with the wheels. Later sold to painter André Derain, after having been given more conventional fixed wings. Engine: 3,257cc 8-cyl. Power: 175bhp. Wheelbase: 298cm.

VOISIN 'VOITURE DE L'AVENIR' Paris, October 1934. Gabriel Voisin's vision of the future, here in scale-model format – complete with diamond-pattern wheel configuration. Engine: air-cooled 4-litre 7-cyl radial. Power: 100bhp. Maximum speed: 112mph.

LE CORBUSIER VOITURE MAXIMUM

BUGATTI 57 S ROADSTER

LE CORBUSIER VOITURE MAXIMUM Paris, March 1935. Project for a compact one-box monocoque four-seater (three-seat front bench and single transverse rear seat). Initially sketched out in 1928 by Le Corbusier, the plans were subsequently put on show as part of a competition to design a popular car organised by the Société des Ingénieurs de l'Automobile. Length: 370cm.

DUBONNET FORD DOLPHIN

MAYBACH SW 35 STROMLINIE (SPOHN)

DUBONNET FORD DOLPHIN Montlhéry, March 1936. One-box aerodynamic proto-type, a five-seater with the driving position ahead of the front axle, conceived by Gustave Chedru and Jean Andreau; access was by two side doors and two in the nose of the car. Plans and sketches were released in October 1935, before the first tests at Montlhéry – where Andre Dubonnét lapped at 174.404kph (108.4mph), with a marked drop in fuel consumption (37 per cent less than a standard Ford with the same 72bhp V8 engine).

MAYBACH SW 35 STROMLINIE (SPOHN) Paris, October 1935. Aerodynamic prototype by Paul Jaray; three were made, the first being sold to boxer Max Schmeling. Engine: 3,817cc 6-cyl. Power: 140bhp at 4,500rpm. Wheelbase: 368cm.

STOUT SCARAB

STOUT SCARAB
Detroit, November 1935.
One-box vehicle conceived as a 'travelling machine' by aircraft manufacturer William Stout: as in an aeroplane fuselage, the cockpit was separated from the passenger area. A handful of examples were sold, in dribs and drabs. The engine was a rear-mounted V8 Ford.

BUGATTI AÉROLITHE

BUGATTI AÉROLITHE
Paris, October 1935.
Coupé anticipating the 57S Atlantic – of which only three examples would be built, between October 1936 and May 1938. Distinguished by the riveted fins on the body and on the crown of the wings. Engine: 3,257cc 8-cyl. Power: 140bhp at 4,500rpm. Wheelbase: 330cm.

PEUGEOT BECAME ONE OF THE EUROPEAN LEADERS IN AERODYNAMICISM WITH THE 1935 LAUNCH OF THE 402. BUT THE FOLLOWING YEAR THE COMPANY ROLLED OUT A PROTOTYPE ANTICIPATING A PROPOSED 1940 MODEL…

Paris, October 1936. At the request of Peugeot, engineer Jean Andreau came up with a completely new body for the 402, just after its launch at the 1935 Paris show. While the first of the Peugeots with the *Fuseau Sochaux* ('Sochaux Streamliner') body styling were just coming onto the market, Peugeot's design offices in the 16th arrondissement of Paris were already beginning their investigations into a hypothetical 1940 model. To this end they called in an eminent engineer from the Arts et Métiers, Jean Andreau, who had an independent design office in Paris, on the Boulevard du Montparnasse. Taking the 402 chassis as his starting point, Jean Andreau concocted an ultra-streamlined body the aerodynamic qualities of which were founded in the realities of scientific research.

The first blueprints for the '402 Andreau' are dated October 1935, but the car only officially appeared at the 1936 Paris show. If the overall shape of the front took in the characteristic radiator cowl of the standard 402, with its close-set headlamps behind a curved grille, in contrast the body was most definitely original. The sides were barrelled, the windscreen panoramic and well raked back, the glasshouse pillarless, and – above all – the rear featured that tailfin that gave the car its futurist flavour. Henri Thomas, Peugeot's in-house stylist, gave a dose of elegance and harmony to these scientifically-evolved lines, based on a not inconsiderable 509cm length and 315cm wheelbase.

Tested in the windtunnel as a scale model, the results were stunning: the Cd went as low as 0.34, while the standard saloon could only manage a 0.68 coefficient of drag. Equipped with the same 55bhp engine as the regular 402, the '1940 model' would be credited with a maximum speed of 87mph rather than the 71.5mph of the normal saloon! That was something of a windfall for Andreau, who according to legend was paid pro-rata on the basis of each extra kilometre per hour his design achieved…

The '1940' 402 served as a rolling test-bed and underwent countless dynamic tests, notably in the hands of racing driver Charles de Cortanze. Various technical innovations were experimented with on the six prototypes ultimately built. Hydraulic brakes and even a V8 engine were tried, on vehicles carring the identification NA8, N4X and N8X. In theory this futuristic saloon was to have been launched for the 1940 model year, but the tragic events of the time decided otherwise. The project was abandoned, but one of the prototypes was saved, and has been preserved by a collector in Provençe.

The two prototypes shown here differ in numerous details. In particular on the car preserved by Hubert Aurant the windscreen is of the 'Vutotal' type, with the pillars covered by the glazing.

DELAGE 12-CYLINDER (LABOURDETTE) Paris, **October 1937**. Prototype created for the French GP. Damaged in testing at Montlhéry in July 1937, the car was nonetheless displayed at the Paris show on the stand of coachbuilder Jean-Henri Labourdette. The 'Vutotal' pillarless-windscreen body was the work of Jean Andreau. Engine: 4,480cc V12. Power: 190bhp at 4,500rpm. Wheelbase: 295cm.

LANCIA APRILIA BERLINETTA (PININ FARINA)

LANCIA APRILIA BERLINETTA (PININ FARINA) Milan, **October 1937**. Pinin Farina developed a streamlined body (Cd 0.39) for Lancia's entries in the 1938 Mille Miglia. Several variants were built, some with fully-enclosed front and rear wheels. Engine: 1,358cc V4. Power: 47bhp at 4,300rpm. Maximum speed: 100mph. Wheelbase: 289cm.

PHANTOM CORSAIR (BOHMANN & SCHWARTZ)

PHANTOM CORSAIR (BOHMANN & SCHWARTZ)
Pasadena, March 1938. Prototype built by Bohmann and Schwartz to a design by ketchup king Rust Heinz. Based on a Cord 810, the car was the star of the film *The Young at Heart*, featuring Paulette Goddard and Douglas Fairbanks. Engine: 4,729cc V8. Power: 190bhp. Weight: 2,200kg. Maximum speed: 118mph.

BUICK Y-JOB

DELAHAYE 165 PHAETON (FIGONI & FALASCHI)

MERCEDES-BENZ 170 H (AVA)

BUICK Y-JOB New **York, January 1939**. Convertible based on the Buick Roadmaster. Designed by George Snyder under the direction of Harley J Earl, it was one of America's first 'dream cars'. The retractable headlamps were replaced by a more conventional arrangement after the war. Engine: 5,244cc Dynaflash straight-eight. Power: 141bhp. Wheelbase: 320cm. Length: 528cm.

MERCEDES-BENZ 170 H (AVA) Berlin, **January 1939**. Aerodynamic one-box prototype conceived by Karl Schlör in association with AVA (Aerodynamische Versuchs-Anstalt) in Göttingen. Based on a rear-engined Mercedes-Benz 170H, the car was windtunnel-tested at Göttingen, recording a Cd of 0.189. Engine: 1,697cc 4-cyl. Power: 38bhp. Length: 432.8cm. Width: 210cm. Height: 147.5cm. Wheelbase: 260cm. Maximum speed: 82mph.

DELAHAYE 165 PHAETON (FIGONI & FALASCHI) Paris, **October 1938**. More than a 'special body', this was a genuine prototype for a prestige car using the mechanicals of the competition 165 model. Engine: 4,496cc V12. Cotal gearbox. Power: 170bhp at 4,500rpm. Wheelbase: 321cm.

CHRYSLER THUNDERBOLT

CHRYSLER THUNDERBOLT New York, January **1939**. Four-seater convertible with an all-enveloping pontoon body featuring retractable headlamps. Built on a Chrysler New Yorker chassis, to a design by Alex Tremulis; six in all were made. Engine: 8-cyl in line. Power: 143bhp.

ASTON MARTIN ATOM

ASTON MARTIN ATOM
Feltham, September 1939. Prototype for a compact four-door saloon. It stood out on account of its tubular spaceframe construction and its independent front suspension. Engine: 1,949cc 4-cyl. Wheelbase: 250.2cm.

CHRYSLER NEWPORT

Indianapolis, May 1941.
The pace car for the Indy 500 in 1941 was this imposing prototype, a twin-cowl phaeton built by Le Baron to a design by Ralph Roberts.

CHRYSLER NEWPORT

MATHIS VL333

BMW 335 K4 (REUTTER)

BMW 335 K4 (REUTTER) **Stuttgart, November 1939.** Last in a line of prototypes (K1 to K4) designed by Wunibald Kamm in conjunction with Stuttgart University's FKFS, an institute set up to research into transportation and engine design. The K-cars were characterised by a chopped-off 'Kamm' tail. Engine: 3,485cc 6-cyl. Power: 90bhp at 3,500rpm. Wheelbase: 298.4cm.

MATHIS VL333 **Paris, October 1946.** Aerodynamic three-wheel city car, with three seats and a fuel consumption of less than 3 litres per 100km (94.2mpg) – hence its name. The streamlined body (Cd 0.22) was designed by Jean Andreau, and the car had front-wheel drive and a four-speed gearbox. Engine: 707cc flat-twin. Power: 15bhp at 3,300rpm. Length: 340cm. Width: 174cm. Wheelbase: 230cm. Weight: 460kg.

ARZENS L'ŒUF

ARZENS L'ŒUF **Paris, June 1943.** Electric-powered urban vehicle created during the Occupation by stylist Paul Arzens; bodied in aluminium, duralinox and plexiglas. Length: 210cm. Width: 125cm. Weight: 350kg.

BRANDT REINE 1950
Paris, October 1948. One-box four-door saloon with emphasis on visibility. Access was either by the door in the nose of the car or by a door at the rear. Engine: 935cc 8-cyl two-stroke. Power: 55/75bhp at 3,000/4,500rpm. Length: 413cm. Width: 183cm. Weight: 550kg.

RENAULT JUVAQUATRE TAXI (FAGET-VARNET)

LANCIA APRILIA (PININ FARINA)

LANCIA APRILIA (PININ FARINA) **Turin, March 1947.** After the Second World War, countless coach-builders busied themselves with creating all-enveloping pontoon bodywork along the lines of Chrysler's Thunderbolt. This was a design by Fedele Bianco for Pinin Farina.

RENAULT JUVAQUATRE TAXI (FAGET-VARNET)
Paris, May 1945. At the design competition for a Paris taxi held in the Bois de Boulogne on 3 May 1945, five proposals were presented. The winner was this one-box design by Escoffier, built by Faget-Varnet to plans laid down by the engineer Jacques Rousseau.

FIAT 500 PANORAMICA (ZAGATO)
Brescia, May 1947. In a continuing quest for more light, Zagato came up with this 'Panoramic' body style, with a glasshouse (side-windows and front screen) cut into the roof. The principle was applied to various chassis.

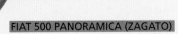

FIAT 500 PANORAMICA (ZAGATO)

BRANDT REINE 1950

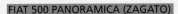

In the midst of post-war reconstruction, the old established Panhard marque was brave enough to project itself into the future and contemplate an aerodynamic saloon for the coming generation...

PANHARD DYNAVIA

Paris, October 1948. The hopes which were sketchily born after the Liberation of France encouraged certain enlightened spirits to conceive motor cars that were to a greater or lesser degree revolutionary. Louis Bionier, responsible for the bodywork of Panhards since 1921, was one of those who reflected on the future of the automobile, and he came up with an aerodynamic saloon that was capable of forming the basis for a future production model. The Dynavia was built on a short wheelbase, which resulted in long overhangs. The body was perfectly ovoid and approximated to the ideal teardrop shape which has always fascinated aerodynamicists. Not a single sharp angle broke up the all-enclosed streamlining, other than the sharp backbone which defined the pointed rear.

In the interior the dashboard itself was rounded and followed the flow of the exterior. But in spite of its uncompromised form, the Dynavia retained adequate room for four people and offered panoramic visibility.

The Dynavia incorporated certain stylised ornamental elements – most notably the front-end treatment, which in one over-wrought assemblage took in the headlamps, the bumpers and the grille for the air intake. On the mechanical side the Dynavia was related to the Dyna which had its début at the 1946 Paris show. It was powered by a 610cc flat-twin developing 28bhp and driving the front wheels. In spite of this modest running gear the Dynavia could reach 80mph.

At the Institut Aérotechnique at Saint-Cyr, the windtunnel turned up a remarkable Cd of 0.171 for the scale model of the Dynavia. In running trim, the operational car registered a more realistic but still excellent drag coefficient of 0.26. Other than its aerodynamic prowess, the Dynavia could boast a much reduced weight, owing to the intensive use of light alloys, notably duralinox.

The unusual lines of the new Dyna Z, which was to appear in 1953, owed much to the audacity of the Dynavia.

Although profoundly futurist, the Dynavia contributed many of its aerodynamic lessons to the Dyna Z introduced for 1954.

RENAULT JUVAQUATRE TAXI

DELAHAYE 175 SIROCCO (FIGONI & FALASCHI)

DELAHAYE 175 SIROCCO (FIGONI & FALASCHI)
Paris, October 1948. Figoni & Falaschi attempted a pontoon style with this heavy-looking offering (in blue and white) presented on the Delahaye stand. Engine: 4,455cc 6-cyl. Power: 140bhp. Wheelbase: 295cm.

RENAULT JUVAQUATRE TAXI **Boulogne-Billancourt, 1949**. One-box Juvaquatre-based Renault prototype with centre-hinged doors. Very much inspired by the Escoffier project that won the 1945 Bois de Boulogne competition to design a Paris taxi, the vehicle was subjected to several months of trials by Renault in the streets of the capital.

ISOTTA-FRASCHINI 8C MONTEROSA

CLAVEAU DESCARTES
Paris, October 1949. As in Paris in 1948 and Geneva in 1949, Emile Claveau again showed his interesting (Cd 0.34) six-seater saloon. With a single-overhead-cam V8, the car featured front-wheel drive and variable-rate all-independent suspension. Engine: 2,292cc V8. Power: 85bhp at 4,200rpm. Length: 497cm. Width: 177cm. Height: 155cm. Wheelbase: 307cm. Weight: 900kg.

ISOTTA-FRASCHINI 8C MONTEROSA **Paris, October 1948**. Prototype created in 1948 to relaunch the Isotta-Fraschini marque; rear-mounted 3.4-litre V8. Six cars were built, to a design by Fabio Luigi Rapi: saloons by Touring and Zagato, a coupé by Touring, and two cabriolets by Boneschi.

WIMILLE-FORD (FAGET-VARNET) **Paris, October 1948**. Forward-looking project created by racing driver Jean-Pierre Wimille, working with stylist Philippe Charbonneaux. The design was remarkable for its unadorned lines, slatted rear window and deep-cut windows, not to mention its three-abreast seating and central driving position. The car's configuration was equally novel, with a mid-mounted Ford engine. Engine: 2,158cc V8. Power: 60bhp. Gearbox: Cotal. Length: 450cm. Width: 170cm. Height: 140cm. Wheelbase: 270cm. Weight: 1,150kg. Maximum speed: 98mph.

MATHIS 666

MATHIS 666 **Paris, October 1948**. Four-door saloon whose body placed great emphasis on a generous glass area. Engine: 2,840cc flat-four. Gearbox: three-speed. Power: 80bhp at 3,900rpm. Length: 447cm. Width: 167cm. Height: 150cm. Wheelbase: 264cm.

CLAVEAU DESCARTES

TASCO **Rosemont, January 1949**. Head of design at Auburn-Cord-Duesenberg from 1929 until 1937 and then part of the Raymond Loewy team from 1944 until 1949, Gordon Buehrig designed this prototype for The American Sports Car Company (TASCO). The wings completely enclosed the wheels and at the front turned with them. The engine was a Mercury V8, and the body was by Derham.

TASCO

WIMILLE-FORD (FAGET-VARNET)

DELAHAYE 175 CABRIOLET (SAOUTCHIK) **Paris, June 1949**. Hanging onto their age-old practices, France's coachbuilders continued to produce vehicles that were often poorly-judged and over-wrought. All the same, some had a certain panache, such as this creation by Saoutchik. Engine: 4,455cc 6-cyl. Power: 140bhp. Wheelbase: 295cm.

DELAHAYE 175 CABRIOLET (SAOUTCHIK)

CHRYSLER K310 (GHIA)

Detroit, January 1951. The first of a series of prototypes designed for Chrysler by Virgil Exner and built by Ghia, this coupé (in pale green and black) was built on a Chrysler Saratoga chassis. The way the headlamps were recessed under a peak turned out to be a much-copied motif. Engine: 5,424cc V8. Power: 180bhp. Length: 560.1cm. Wheelbase: 318.8cm.

CHRYSLER K310 (GHIA)

ROVER JET 1

Silverstone, March 1950. The first car in history to be powered by a gas-turbine (mid-mounted, and developing 100bhp), this was a two-seater roadster based on the Rover 75, and designed under the direction of Frank Bell. JET 1 was shown in New York in April 1950, and went on to clock 151.96mph at Jabbeke in 1952.

RENAULT 4 CV VUTOTAL (LABOURDETTE)

RENAULT 4 CV VUTOTAL (LABOURDETTE)

Paris, October 1950. Convertible created by Jean-Henri Labourdette to showcase his 'Vutotal' approach to the question of visibility; originated in the 1930s, it did away with the screen pillars. The headlamps on this exercise were housed behind a shaped glass cover and the body had somewhat odd proportions. Engine: 760cc 4-cyl. Power: 21bhp.

ROVER JET 1

VOISIN BISCOOTER

Paris, October 1950. Prototype for an ultra-economical and rudimentary two-seater. Front-wheel-drive, and powered by an air-cooled two-stroke Gnome & Rhône engine. A developed version of the Biscooter would be made in Spain by Autonacional.

GENERAL MOTORS LE SABRE

Chicago, February 1951. This two-seater convertible is one of the most famous dream cars in history. In full-blown aero-military fantasy, its name refers to a fighter aircraft. Engine: 3,526cc V8, supercharged. Power: 335bhp at 5,200rpm. Length: 510cm. Height: 127cm. Weight: 1,752kg.

VOISIN BISCOOTER

WIMILLE-FORD (FAGET-VARNET)

WIMILLE-FORD (FAGET-VARNET)

Paris, October 1950. For its second appearance at the Paris show, in 1949, the Wimille lost its central headlamp and gained thicker bumpers. For its third showing the car would further change and be given four headlamps. But the death of Jean-Pierre Wimille in 1949 would put paid to this fascinating project.

BENTLEY MARK VI (FACEL-METALLON)

BENTLEY MARK VI (FACEL-METALLON)

Paris, October 1951. The elegance of the future Facel-Véga could already be seen in the purity of line of this MkVI (chassis B98KM) bodied by Jean Daninos. Engine: 4,257cc 6-cyl. Power: 122bhp. Wheelbase: 304.8cm.

BUICK XP-300

Chicago, February 1951. Aluminium-bodied two-seater convertible, fuelled with a petrol-methanol mix. Equipment included an adjustable steering wheel and an integral jacking system. Engine: 3.5-litre V8 with supercharger. Power: 355bhp. Transmission: Dynaflow. Weight: 1,423kg.

BUICK XP-300

GENERAL MOTORS LE SABRE

AT THE BEGINNING OF THE 1950s, THE CAR INDUSTRY START TO FLIRT AGAIN
WITH THE AVIATION WORLD. THE JET ENGINES POWERING AIRCRAFT INSPIRED
A HANDFUL OF DREAMERS...

Paris, October 1952. At the dawn of the 1950s the motor car entered anew a period of fascination with the world of aviation. Aeronautical influences crossed an unexpected threshold, all the same, when engineers pondered on powering roadgoing vehicles with a gas-turbine – with the English firm Rover, in 1950, the first to adapt a gas-turbine to a car.

In France the pioneer of this form of propulsion was Jean-Albert Grégoire. Promoter of front-wheel drive in the 1920s, and of light alloys

and aerodynamicism in the 1940s, Grégoire was curious about all new technologies. In company with fellow engineer Maurice Moisy he turned to Socéma (Société de Construction et d'Equipements Mécaniques pour l'Aviation) in order to develop the first French car equipped with a gas-turbine. In this venture he was supported by Paul Piaton, director of the Compagnie Electro-Mécanique of which Socéma was an offshoot, and by Péchiney, who controlled Aluminium Française. The Socéma-Grégoire was powered by a 100bhp turbine engine. Called

Cematurbo, this unit comprised a turbo-compressor turning at 45,000rpm and a power turbine turning at 25,000rpm, coupled to a reduction gear operating a transmission shaft turning at 5,000rpm. This linked to a rear-mounted clutch connected to a Cotal gearbox and a Telma speed-reducer placed ahead of the differential. For its running gear the Socéma-Grégoire borrowed from the Hotchkiss-Grégoire, but with the cast-aluminium structure being internal rather than external. The car's lines were well-balanced despite the long front overhang

SOCËMA-GREGOIRE

caused by the gas-turbine's position ahead of the axle; the circular air intake symbolised the presence of the jet engine. The aerodynamic body (claimed Cd 0.19) was in aluminium, and with a length of 460cm and height of 135cm it was relatively compact.

For more than a decade prototypes with gas-turbine power flourished everywhere – in Italy with the Fiat Turbina (1954); in France with the Renault Etoile Filante (Paris, 1956); and above all in the US, with GM's Firebirds (1954–64) and Chrysler's Turbine Cars (1955–63).

With its elegant and practical lines, the Socéma-Grégoire was very different from the General Motors gas-turbine cars, with their detailing borrowed from aviation and aerospace…

PACKARD PAN AMERICAN

ALFA ROMEO DISCO VOLANTE (TOURING)

Monza, October 1952. Racing barchetta built on chassis 1900C52-2000 (no.001). The car's ovoid profile led to its being nicknamed 'the flying saucer'. Never entered in competition, it remained a styling study, and is preserved in the Alfa Romeo museum in Arese. Engine: 1,997cc 4-cyl. Power: 158bhp at 6,500rpm. Wheelbase: 222cm. Weight: 735kg. Maximum speed: 136mph.

ALFA ROMEO DISCO VOLANTE (TOURING)

LANCIA PF 200 SPIDER (PININ FARINA)

PACKARD PAN AMERICAN **New York, March 1952**. Convertible with classic lines, built by the Henney Motor Company to a design by Richard Arbib, working under the direction of Edward Macauley. Predecessor to Packard's Balboa of 1953. Engine: 5,358cc 8-cyl. Power: 175bhp.

LANCIA PF 200 SPIDER (PININ FARINA) **Turin, April 1952**. Two-seater roadster designed by Adriano Rabbone and based on the Lancia Aurelia B52. The car's stripped-down linear profile and its circular jet-engine grille stylishly melded aeronautical motifs. Engine: 1,991cc V6. Power: 70bhp at 4,500rpm. Wheelbase: 291cm.

FORD X-100 **Paris, October 1952**. A sedanca-style cabriolet of which certain details anticipated future production models – notably the rear, which was borrowed for the 1962 Thunderbird. The exterior was by Joe Oros, the interior by John Najjar.

FORD X-100

PEGASO Z-102 'EL DOMINICANO'

CHRYSLER C-200

Chicago, February 1952. Conventional convertible (presented in pale green and black) derived from the Chrysler K-310; styled by Virgil Exner and built by Ghia. Length: 560.1cm. Wheelbase: 318.8cm.

CHRYSLER C-200

PEGASO Z-102 'EL DOMINICANO' **Paris, October 1952**. Unique two-seater coupé, built in Pegaso's own workshops on chassis 1500121 and purchased by Dominican Republic dictator Rafael Trujillo y Molina. The car's aggressive lines finished in an impressive bubbleback rear. Exhibited subsequently at the February 1953 World Motor Sports Show in New York. Engine: 2,815cc V8. Power: 170bhp. Wheelbase: 234cm.

FIAT-ABARTH 1400 COUPÉ (BERTONE) **Turin, April 1952**. Coupé built on Abarth chassis, using Fiat 1400 mechanicals. One of the first creations of Franco Scaglione (who used the name 'Frasca'), it was characteristically bold and voluptuous.

LANCIA PF 200 COUPÉ (PININ FARINA) **Paris, October 1952**. Coupé based on the PF 200 spider shown at Turin: the panoramic glasshouse further developed the aeronautical styling theme. A cabriolet was also produced, along similar lines. Engine: 1,991cc V6. Power: 70bhp at 4,500rpm. Wheelbase: 291cm.

LANCIA PF 200 COUPÉ (PININ FARINA)

FIAT-ABARTH 1400 COUPÉ (BERTONE)

LINCOLN XL-500

Chicago, March 1953. Coupé exhibited by Lincoln-Mercury at the Chicago Automobile Show. Plastic body designed by John Najjar. Engine: 5.2-litre V8. Power: 205bhp. Length: 549.3cm. Width: 207cm. Height: 144.6cm. Wheelbase: 312.4cm.

LINCOLN XL-500

BUICK WILDCAT

New York, 1953. Sporting two-seater convertible of no great distinction. The 1953 General Motors 'Motorama' also featured the Cadillac Le Mans and Orleans and the Pontiac Parisienne. Engine: 5.3-litre V8. Power: 150bhp.

ALFA ROMEO BAT 5 (BERTONE)

ALFA ROMEO BAT 5 (BERTONE) **Turin, April 1953**. The first of Bertone's Berlinetta Aerodinamica Tecnica cars – a futuristic design by Franco Scaglione (1917–1980), based on the Alfa Romeo 1900 Sprint. Engine: 1,884cc 4-cyl. Power: 100bhp at 5,500rpm. Wheelbase: 250cm.

BUICK WILDCAT

FORD SYRTIS

Dearborn, May 1953. Taking up an idea from French coachbuilder Pourtout, Ford developed an electrically-retractable hardtop called the 'Roof-o-Matic', and it was tried out on the Syrtis before being offered on the production Fairlane Skyliner of 1957.

FORD SYRTIS

PEGASO Z-102 THRILL (TOURING)

PEGASO Z-102 THRILL (TOURING) **Turin, April 1953**. Two-seat berlinetta coupé ultimately owned by Eva Peron. Designed by Federico Formenti, under Felice Bianchi Anderloni, it featured an original rear treatment with fins flowing out from the B-post. Engine: 2,815cc V8. Power: 170bhp. Wheelbase: 234cm.

DODGE FIREARROW (GHIA) **Turin, April 1953**. Roadster initially shown as a mock-up, but later made into a rolling prototype (Firearrow II) for 1954's 'Harmony on Wheels' exhibition; designed by Virgil Exner. Wheelbase: 292.1cm.

DODGE FIREARROW (GHIA)

CHRYSLER D'ÉLÉGANCE (GHIA) **Detroit, August 1953**. One of Virgil Exner's most successful and most famous designs. The linking together of the sill swage and the rear wing was a striking motif that was to reappear on the Volkswagen Karmann-Ghia. The elegance of the design derived from the relative proportions of the glasshouse and the lower structure. Under the bonnet was a 'Fire Power' V8.

DE SOTO ADVENTURER (GHIA) **Detroit, October 1953**. 2+2 coupé by Virgil Exner. A development of the same design by Ghia's Mario Savonuzzi was shown, as the Adventurer II, at the 1954 Turin show. Engine: 4.5 litre V8. Power: 170bhp. Length: 482.1cm. Wheelbase: 281.9cm.

CHRYSLER D'ÉLÉGANCE (GHIA)

DeSOTO ADVENTURER (GHIA)

THE INITIALS 'BAT' DON'T STAND FOR BATMOBILE... HOWEVER, THESE TORTURED LINES TOOK THE MOTOR CAR INTO A FRIGHTENING FICTIONAL UNIVERSE. WITH THE BATS BERTONE JOINED THE ARISTOCRACY OF THE STYLING WORLD.

ALFA ROMEO BAT 7 (BERTONE)

Turin, **April 1954**. At the beginning of the 1950s the renaissance of car styling originated in Italy. In the Italy of the common man, as depicted in the films of Vittorio de Sica or Federico Fellini, in *The Bicycle Thief* or *I Vitelloni*, Fiat responded to the needs of a nation still suffering from the tension between the industrialised North and the neglected South. The motor car was the stuff of dreams for a whole country still in the throes of reconstruction. Ferrari, Maserati, Lancia and Alfa Romeo had the coachbuilders as their accomplices…and these enterprises struck out in a new direction. To survive, they had to abandon being artisans and enter the industrial age. The industrial beginnings of Bertone, a concern that had begun life in 1912, date from 1953, when the American millionnaire Wacky Arnolt ordered a series of roadsters on the Bristol chassis.

The transalpine stylists refashioned in their own way the aeronautical fantasies, the taste for excess and the love of ornamentation that inspired their American contemporaries. By means of his 'BAT' series (Berlinetta Aerodinamica Tecnica), Bertone served up his own vision of an automotive dream fuelled by aviation imagery. These prototypes were designed by Franco Scaglione, one of the most brilliant stylists of his generation. The Alfa 1900 mechanicals were wrapped in curled wings ending in distorted fins. A true 'dream car' in the sense in which this was meant in the 1950s, BAT 7 swung between lyricism and naïvity, with its frankly simplistic detailing borrowed from the world of aviation, its over-the-top fins, and its air intakes suggesting the power of a jet engine. Thanks to the talent of Franco Scaglione, the language became poetic, the scrolls of the rear contracting as if they were the wings of a frightened bird. Despite their lack of elegance, the Bertone BATs serve to bear precious witness to the temptations to which stylists and designers of all eras have been victim.

The second of the three BAT cars, BAT 7 is characterised by its long rear wings which turn in on the tail-spine.

OLDSMOBILE 88 CUTLASS

PACKARD PANTHER DAYTONA

OLDSMOBILE 88 CUTLASS New York, January 1954. Sporting coupé with slatted rear window; copper paint finish. Oldsmobile also showed another prototype as part of its Motorama display – the F88 convertible. Engine: 5.3-litre V8. Power: 250bhp. Length: 478.6cm. Width: 130.8cm. Wheelbase: 279.4cm.

BUICK WILDCAT II

BUICK WILDCAT II New York, January 1954. Two-seat roadster in blue distinguished by its original front wing treatment and its panoramic windscreen. The other stars of the GM Motorama exhibition were Buick's Landau, Cadillac's El Camino and Espada, Pontiac's Strato-Streak and Bonneville Special, and Chevrolet's Corvair and Nomad. Engine: 5.3-litre V8. Power: 220bhp. Length: 434cm. Width: 120cm. Wheelbase: 254cm.

MERCURY XM-800

MERCURY XM-800 Dearborn, 1954. Conventional coupé previewing Lincoln's styling for 1956. From 1949 until 1961 George Walker was in charge of Ford styling, and he was happier studying proposed production vehicles than conceiving forward-looking prototypes…

FORD FX-ATMOS Chicago, March 1954. Futurist vehicle using the most obvious styling devices to ape the aviation world: rear fins, glass cockpit-cover, after-burners, radar… The plastic body was in the colours of the stars-and-stripes – red and blue on a white background…

PACKARD PANTHER DAYTONA New York, February 1954. Convertible presented at the New York International Motor Show. The body was in plastic, on the ugly side, and didn't have much stylistic interest. From 1951 until 1957 Packard's design team was led by Richard Teague. 275bhp engine.

FERRARI 375 MM COUPÉ SPÉCIALE (PININ FARINA)

FERRARI 375 MM COUPÉ SPÉCIALE (PININ FARINA) Paris, October 1954. Two-seat coupé made for Roberto Rossellini on 375 MM chassis number 0456AM. Aldo Brovarone's design was characterised by its flying-buttress rear quarters and inset rear window. Single-cam 4,522cc V12 developing 340bhp; 260cm wheelbase.

MASERATI A6GCS BERLINETTA (PININ FARINA)

MASERATI A6GCS BERLINETTA (PININ FARINA) Turin, April 1954. Two-seat berlinetta based on the chassis of the A6 GCS racer. The first made (car number 2057) is recognisable by its dipped waistline. Three other prototypes were built on the same theme. Engine: 1,985cc six-cylinder developing 160bhp.

GENERAL MOTORS FIREBIRD New York, January 1954. Futurist prototype unambiguously resembling a space-rocket on four wheels. This machine also caused a sensation in France, when it was displayed at the 1954 Paris motor show. Engine: Whirlfire gas-turbine. Power 375bhp at 26,000rpm. Length: 556cm. Width: 203cm. Height: 104cm. Wheelbase: 254cm. Weight: 1107kg.

GENERAL MOTORS FIREBIRD

FORD FX-ATMOS

GMC L'UNIVERSELLE New York, January 1955. Anticipatory MPV-like re-jigging of the delivery van. A decade before the hippy generation, General Motors stylists gave this van a character orientated more towards luxury, sportiness and leisure activities.

LaSALLE II SEDAN

GMC L'UNIVERSELLE

LaSALLE II SEDAN **New York, January 1955**. Four-door pillarless saloon designed by Carl Renner under the direction of Harley Earl. GM's other creations for Motorama 1955 were the Chevrolet Biscayne, Pontiac Strato Chief, La Salle II Sport Coupé, Oldsmobile 88 Delta, Cadillac Eldorado Brougham and Buick Wildcat III. Length: 457cm. Height: 126cm. Wheelbase: 274.3cm.

LINCOLN INDIANAPOLIS (BOANO)

LINCOLN INDIANAPOLIS (BOANO) **Turin, April 1955**. Orange-hued coupé designed by former Ghia styling chief Mario Felice Boano, who between 1954 and 1957 ran an independent studio before heading Fiat's styling department. At the same time as he exhibited the Indianapolis, Boano also showed his Chrysler Special Corsaire.

LINCOLN FUTURA **New York, April 1955**. High-camp futurist, this prototype, designed by William M Schmidt and built by Ghia, featured a hinged double-bubble transparent cockpit cover. It was later adapted to form the Batmobile for the famous TV series.

LINCOLN FUTURA

CHRYSLER STREAMLINE / GILDA (GHIA) **Turin, April 1955**. Futuristic coupé which was the object of aerodynamic studies at the Turin Politecnico; the wedge styling by Mario Savonuzzi featured an ultra-low front rising to a sharply-finned rear. Given the name Gilda, the mock-up was sent to the Ford museum in Dearborn; today it is in California's Blackhawk Collection.

CHRYSLER STREAMLINE / GILDA (GHIA)

GAYLORD GLADIATOR (SPOHN)

ALFA ROMEO BAT 9 (BERTONE) **Turin, April 1955**. Last of the three 'BAT' cars, this one is more classical in shape, with cropped wings, fixed headlamps and more conventionally Alfa front. Again, the Alfa Romeo 1900 was the car's basis. Engine: 1,975cc twin-cam 4-cyl. Power: 115bhp at 5,500rpm. Wheelbase: 250cm.

GAYLORD GLADIATOR (SPOHN) **Paris, October 1955**. Project for a luxury coupé initiated by Jim and Edward Gaylord, and powered by a 5.4-litre Chrysler V8; interesting post-modern design by Brook Stevens Associates. Five examples were produced, three with retractable hardtops.

ALFA ROMEO BAT 9 (BERTONE)

CHRYSLER FALCON (GHIA) **New York, April 1955**. Elegant convertible of which three examples built. De Soto 'Hemi' and PowerFlite transmission. Engine: 4,524cc V8. Power: 170bhp at 4,400rpm. Length: 462.3cm. Width: 173.5cm. Height: 130cm. Wheelbase: 266.7cm. Weight: 1,485kg.

CHRYSLER FALCON (GHIA)

IN THE SHADOW OF HIS SUMPTUOUS GRAND TOURING COUPÉS, PININ FARINA
PRESENTED A VEHICLE ORIENTATED TOWARDS THE LEISURE MARKET. THIS
FORWARD-LOOKING MACHINE WAS LESS FUTILE THAN MIGHT APPEAR.

Paris, October 1956. In the middle of the 1950s Pinin Farina was one of the most respected of coachbuilders. From his collabor-ation with Ferrari had already emerged some genuine masterpieces, among which was a series of competition coupés on the 250MM,

340MM and 375MM chassis – not to forget the convertible created for King Leopold on 375MM chassis 0488AM.

Pinin Farina also distinguished himself with the Lancia Florida duo. The first car was shown at Turin in 1955. It was a coupé which already

brought together the stylistic details that would immortalise the model: stripped-bare dihedral sides pressed with a mid-panel crease that played with the effects of light, pillarless side-windows, and a C-post whose line flowed into a fin on the rear wing, the rear window being recessed

FIAT EDEN ROC (PININ FARINA)

between these buttresses. The two-tone paint (white and marine blue) helped to separate visually the infrastructure from the superstructure.

The second Florida was shown at the October 1955 Paris salon. It was similar to the Turin car, but had four doors opening to reveal a passenger compartment unimpeded by any central pillar. This design was taken up without much modification for the production Lancia Flaminia which was launched at the 1957 Geneva show.

Meanwhile Pinin Farina wasn't idle, and he showed various other proposals during the 1956 season. At Brussels there was a third version of the Florida. At Turin in April the prolific coachbuilder unveiled two prototypes: the white Superflow based on the Alfa Romeo 6C-3500 and the green Palm Beach based on the Nash Ramber. Finally, beside the Palm Beach, the red-with-white-stripes Superflow II and the first of the spectacular Ferrari 410 Superfasts (chassis 02207SA), Pinin Farina showed a car which even if it was his smallest of the year, was nevertheless the most original: for the first time a constructor took the deliberate decision to develop a car specifically for leisure use.

The Eden Roc was based on the mechanicals of the Fiat 600 Multipla, recently shown at the 1956 Brussels salon. This remarkable vehicle was an ultra-compact (353cm) one-box design capabable of carrying six adults. The Eden Roc kept the Multipla's engine (633cc and 22bhp), its forward-control driving position and its 200cm wheelbase.

Entirely open, denuded of doors and equipped with a wraparound rear bench seat made of wood strips, the Eden Roc was dedicated to summertime and to the beach, to the shores of the Italian Riviera and the Côte d'Azur, kissed by the sun and by holiday dollars. Henry Ford received an Eden Roc, even though the climate in Detroit attracted rather fewer starlets than that of La Croisette…

Based on the clever Multipla, the Eden Roc was a car that was as charming as it was rudimentary. It was specifically designed for cruising the beaches.

BUICK CENTURION

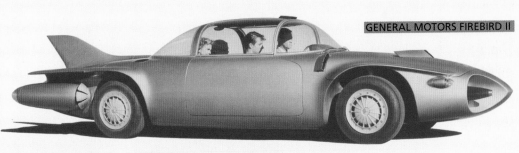

GENERAL MOTORS FIREBIRD II

PONTIAC CLUB DE MER

FIAT-ABARTH 750 SPERIMENTALE (VIGNALE)

BUICK CENTURION

New York, January 1956. Four-seater coupé designed by Chuck Jordan under the direction of Harley Earl. The view to the rear was by a television screen. Also shown at the 1956 GM Motorama (Waldorf Astoria hotel, 19–24 January 1956) was the Chevrolet Impala concept. Engine: V8. Power: 325bhp. Length: 542.3cm. Width: 186.7cm. Height: 136.4cm. Wheelbase: 299.7cm.

PONTIAC CLUB DE MER

New York, January 1956. Futuristic roadster still very much aerospace-influenced, with its double-cowl cockpit, profiled nose and central tailfin; powered by 300bhp Strato-Streak V8, linked to automatic transmission. De Dion rear axle. Length: 457cm. Height: 97cm.

GENERAL MOTORS FIREBIRD II **New York, January 1956**. Futurist four-seater, and second in the series of Firebirds; gas-turbine power was retained, this time with 200bhp. Electro-magnetic four-speed gearbox. Precursor of the XP-500. Length: 585cm. Height: 130cm. Wheelbase: 300cm.

ROVER T3

CHRYSLER PLAINSMAN

ROVER T3

London, October 1956. Two-seater coupé with gas-turbine engine above rear suspension; technical director Spen King, under Maurice Wilks. Plastic body designed by David Bache. 110bhp gas-turbine and four-wheel drive; maximum speed 100mph. Length: 380.6cm. Width: 150.6cm. Height: 134.7cm. Wheelbase: 238.4cm.

CHRYSLER PLAINSMAN

Chicago, January 1956. Estate-car concept, with rearmost of three bench seats facing backwards and folding flat to increase floorspace. The same year the Chrysler Norseman disappeared in the shipwreck of the liner *Andrea Doria*, on 26 July 1956. Engine: 4.3-litre V8. Power: 115bhp. Wheelbase: 292.1cm.

FORD MYSTÈRE

Dearborn, 1956. Styling exercise by the Ford Motor Company. At the rear could be either a conventional engine or a gas-turbine, the Ford press release said, hedging its bets. The gullwing side moulding was adopted on production Fords of the time.

FIAT-ABARTH 750 SPERIMENTALE (VIGNALE)

Geneva, March 1956. Compact sporting coupé based on the Fiat 600. Two-box (red and black) body with 'monovolume' front. A second car, built for the 1957 Geneva show, took part in that year's Mille Miglia. Engine: 747cc 4-cyl. Power: 41.5bhp at 5,500rpm. Maximum speed: 104mph.

FORD MYSTÈRE

ALFA ROMEO SPORTIVA (BERTONE)

ALFA ROMEO SPORTIVA (BERTONE). **Turin, April 1956**. Splendid coupé designed by Franco Scaglione for Bertone – its style would inspire the Giulietta Sprint. Two made: both survive. Engine: 1,997cc 4-cyl. Power: 138bhp at 6,500rpm. De Dion rear axle. Wheelbase: 220cm. Weight: 915kg. Maximum speed: 137mph.

CHRYSLER 400 (GHIA)
CHRYSLER 400 (GHIA)

CHRYSLER 400 (GHIA)
Turin, October 1957.
Aerodynamic coupé developing the styling themes of the Gilda (Turin 1955), Dart, and Dart Apribile (Turin 1956), as taken up again on the Dart A498 (Turin 1958). Body and upholstery in yellow and black.

FIAT SPIAGETTA (VIGNALE)

OLDSMOBILE GOLDEN ROCKET

OLDSMOBILE GOLDEN ROCKET

FIAT SPIAGETTA (VIGNALE) **Turin, October 1957**. Beach car based on the Fiat 600 Multipla. In contrast to Pinin Farina's Eden Roc, the passengers sat on bench seats made of plastic and had the protection of a roof.

CHEVROLET CORVETTE XP-SS

OLDSMOBILE GOLDEN ROCKET **Paris, October 1957**. Yet another dream car drawing on spaceship and military imagery, the Golden Rocket was first seen in New York in January 1956, but was nonetheless one of the stars of the Paris salon more than a year and a half later. The roof opened in two halves to help entry. Engine: 6.1-litre V8. Power: 275bhp. Length: 500cm..

CHEVROLET CORVETTE XP-SS **Sebring, March 1957**. A competition car before becoming a styling exercise, the XP-SS first ran at Sebring. Magnesium-alloy body, moly-steel tube chassis and De Dion rear axle conceived by Zora Arkus-Duntov. Engine: 4,638cc V8. Power: 310bhp at 6,200rpm. Wheelbase: 234cm. Weight: 845kg.

BMW 507 (PICHON-PARAT) **Paris, October 1957**. Coupé based on a BMW 507, designed by Raymond Loewy and built by Pichon-Parat, coachbuilders in Sens, near Paris. The lines anticipated the 1962 Studebaker Avanti. Engine: 3,168cc V8. Power: 150bhp at 5,000rpm. Wheelbase: 248cm.

FIAT-ABARTH 750 (PININ FARINA)

BMW 507 (PICHON-PARAT)

BUICK LIDO (PININ FARINA) **Paris, October 1957**. Coupé with part-opening roof to aid access. White coachwork with black roof; turquoise upholstery. Engine: 6,554cc V8. Wheelbase: 309.8cm.

FIAT-ABARTH 750 (PININ FARINA) **Geneva, March 1957**. Single-seater with streamlined aluminium body. Holder of several speed records at Monza, notably in the hands of Paul Frère (in excess of 125mph over 200 miles in October 1957). Preserved in the Abarth Gallery, near Lake Yamanaka, Japan. Engine: 747cc Bialbero 4-cyl. Power: 60bhp at 7,600rpm. Length: 511cm. Width: 161.5cm. Height: 104cm. Wheelbase: 228cm. Weight: 510kg.

BUICK LIDO (PININ FARINA)

STANGUELLINI 1200 SPIDER (BERTONE) **Turin, October 1957**. Roadster designed by Franco Scaglione, based on a Fiat 1200 modified by Stanguellini. Engine: 1,200cc 4-cyl. Power: 60bhp. Maximum speed: 100mph.

STANGUELLINI 1200 SPIDER (BERTONE)

Revved up by the conquest of space that was opposing the east to the west, the all-conquering US multiplied its propaganda operations to show off its power. The Firebird was part of this process.

GENERAL MOTORS FIREBIRD III

Costa Mesa, December 1958. The President of General Motors declared "The new Firebird III contains more ideas in terms of style and technology than its two predecessors, Firebird I and Firebird II". Indeed so. The president believed in his power, the power of General Motors, and the power of all America itself. The military connotations of American dream cars were not innocent. The aeronautical or aerospace references weren't made as a way of heralding improbable mechanical mutants, but as a means of celebrating the merits of American technology.

In contrast to the special bodies shown by the Europeans, American 'dream cars' weren't seen as having an eternal life, in an artistic perspective, but as having a built-in obsolescence. The dream didn't have the same meaning on both sides of the Atlantic. American society was based around the specific idea of creating that of which other countries dreamt. When General Motors showed Firebird III, America was already preparing to conquer space, whereas the space fantasies of Europe were still literary: the Old Continent lived with the memories of Jules Verne and HG Wells, the United States with the promises held out by NASA.

But despite the terrifying visions of George Orwell, the future carried with it great hopes.

The Firebird, the third of the name, first turned a wheel at the GM test track at Costa Mesa, outside Los Angeles in California. A 'Whirlfire' gas-turbine was set at the rear to drive the wheels, and was now pushing out 225bhp. In the car's nose was a small internal-combustion engine, developing 10bhp, to power the auxiliaries.

A single control was positioned on the centre console. This 'Unicontrol' handle allowed one to accelerate (by pushing it forward), brake (by pulling it rearwards), and steer (by making the appropriate gesture to the left or right). Pivoting this device enabled selection of the correct gear ('Park', 'Drive' or reverse). Amongst the other accessories there was electronic speed control, remote opening of the doors, and a gadget allowing the headlamps to switch on automatically.

This is not to forget, of course, the body with its countless fins and wings, which seemed as if they had sprouted naturally from the body…

As a counterpoint to dreams of the conquest of space, America came up with some fantastic machines, untethered to reality and frequently despairingly naïve. The idea of the 'dream car' was never as brilliantly demonstrated as with the Firebird III.

TRIUMPH TR3 COUPÉ (VIGNALE)

CADILLAC CABRIOLET (PININ FARINA)

CADILLAC CABRIOLET (PININ FARINA) **Paris, October 1958**. After the coupé shown at the 1958 Geneva motor show, Pinin Farina presented a Cadillac cabriolet at the Paris salon – the car having silver-grey paint and a red interior. These special bodies were created to mark the industrial co-operation which brought General Motors and the Italian styling house together for the manufacture of the 1958 Eldorado Brougham. Engine: 6,388cc V8. Power: 345bhp at 4,800rpm.

TRIUMPH TR3 COUPÉ (VIGNALE) **Geneva, March 1958**. Pretty coupé based on the Triumph TR3, styled by Giovanni Michelotti and anticipating the Triumph Italia made as a limited run by Vignale from 1959 until 1962.

FIAT 1100 GIARDINETTA (GHIA)

FIAT 1100 GIARDINETTA (GHIA) **Turin, November 1958**. In the same spirit as Pinin Farina's 1958 Austin A40 and his earlier Fiat 1100 TV estate of 1955, this styling exercise explored the idea of a compact two-box saloon with tailgate. The fusion between saloon and estate was up and running. Engine: 1,089cc 4-cyl. Power: 43bhp. Wheelbase: 234cm.

FORD LA GALAXIE

FORD LA GALAXIE

Dearborn, 1958. Coupé with hideously tortured lines and all the usual childish science-fiction gizmos – a cockpit worthy of a fighter-plane, no steering-wheel of course, an electronic alarm system, a radar to warn for obstacles, and an information screen. Length: 567.9cm. Height: 131.6cm. Wheelbase: 320cm.

ARBEL SYMETRIC

Geneva, March 1958. Saloon based on the concept-car created by the Loubières brothers and already seen in 1951. The sliding doors disappear into the roof and the floor. The blurb was tongue-in-cheek enticing: a body in 'polystic', an 'Electric-Drive' transmission, 'Thermogum' suspension, and a static 'Génestafuel' gas or 'Génestatom' nuclear generator… Length: 500cm. Width: 180cm.

FIAT 1200 CABRIOLET (GHIA)

ARBEL SYMETRIC

LANCIA RAGGIO AZZURO V2 (VIGNALE) **Geneva, March 1958**. Coupé designed by Giovanni Michelotti, and based on a Lancia Aurelia modified by Nardi. A development of the styling theme of the 1954 Fiat Demon Rouge and the first Raggio Azzuro (Turin, 1955).

FIAT 1200 CABRIOLET (GHIA) **Turin, November 1958**. This modest cabriolet is one of the first creations of Sergio Sartorelli, a graduate engineer of the Turin Polytechnic who joined Ghia in 1956 and went on to be styling chief from 1960 until 1963. Engine: 1,221cc 4-cyl. Power: 55bhp. Wheelbase: 234cm.

LANCIA RAGGIO AZZURO V2 (VIGNALE)

SCIMITAR HARDTOP CONVERTIBLE (REUTTER)

FERRARI SUPERAMERICA SPECIAL (PININ FARINA)

SCIMITAR HARDTOP CONVERTIBLE (REUTTER) **Geneva, March 1959**. Prototypes ordered in three forms by the Olin Aluminium Corporation: Hardtop Convertible Coupé, station wagon with sliding roof, and 'town car' Convertible. Designed by Brooks Stevens, and built on a Chrysler New Yorker chassis. Engine: 6,771cc V8. Power: 350bhp at 4,600rpm. Gearbox: TorqueFlite 3-speed automatic. Length: 548.6cm. Width: 186.7cm. Height: 146cm. Wheelbase: 322.6cm.

FERRARI SUPERAMERICA SPECIAL (PININ FARINA) **Turin, October 1959.** Coupé built for Giovanni Agnelli on chassis 1517SA. Original frontal treatment by Adriano Rabbone, under the direction of Francesco Martinengo (head of Pinin Farina styling from 1952 until 1972). Engine: 3,967cc V12. Power: 340bhp. Wheelbase: 242cm.

TALBOT STAR SIX

TALBOT STAR SIX **Paris, October 1959**. Project created by Virgil Exner Jr for Simca, which had just bought the Talbot firm. The adventurous lines hide the ancient mechanicals of a Simca Eight! Engine: 1,090cc 4-cyl. Power: 80bhp. Length: 475cm. Width: 176cm. Height: 116cm. Weight: 700kg. Maximum speed: 120mph.

SIMCA FULGUR **Geneva, March 1959**. This futuristic prototype piled on the techno-trickery: electric power rechargeable electro-magnetically via an in-road rail, radar, electronic 'brain', retractable front wheels, gyroscopes to balance the car, and a vee'd rear fin. Much ado about nothing.

SELENE (GHIA)

SELENE (GHIA) **Turin, October 1959**. As part of its studies for Renault, Ghia came up with this rear-engined cab-forward prototype with its huge passenger compartment; the rear seats, for four people, faced each other. The steering wheel could be positioned either on the left or on the right. Length: 512cm. Width: 183cm. Height: 132cm. Wheelbase: 269.2cm.

SIMCA FULGUR

CADILLAC CYCLONE

CADILLAC CYCLONE

CADILLAC CYCLONE **New York, 1959**. Aeronautical imagery just wouldn't go away. On this concept car you found the inevitable hinged glass cockpit-cover, this time linked to sliding doors, while the fins were hardly more extravagant than those of the Cadillac Eldorado Brougham – which was a production car. Engine: 6.4-litre V8. Power: 350bhp.

CADILLAC STARLIGHT (PININ FARINA)

CADILLAC STARLIGHT (PININ FARINA) **Paris, October 1959**. Continuing its collaboration with Cadillac, Pinin Farina came up with this coupé with fully glazed roof. The side treatment, with two swages parting as they go rearwards, would be taken up on Farina's Peugeot 404 cabriolet.

ALFA ROMÉO 3500 SPYDER SUPER SPORT (PININ FARINA)

ALFA ROMÉO 3500 SPYDER SUPER SPORT (PININ FARINA) **Geneva, March 1959**. One of the eight examples of the 6C-3000 CM (chassis 0128) was entrusted to Pinin Farina, which transformed it into the Superflow (Turin, 1956), the Superflow II (Paris, 1956), and finally the Spyder Super Sport. Engine: 6-cyl 3,495cc. Power: 246bhp at 6,500rpm. Wheelbase: 225cm.

FOR SEVERAL YEARS CERTAIN ENLIGHTENED STYLISTS IMAGINED THEY COULD CHANGE THE COURSE OF HISTORY THROUGH DEVELOPING FUTURISTIC DEVICES WITH FORWARD-CONTROL CABS…

LA VOITURE QUI DEVANCE LE TEMPS ET QUI DONNE AUJOURD'HUI UNE DEMONSTRATION RATIONELLEMENT REALISÉE DE LA VOITURE DE DEMAIN

GHIA SELENE SECONDA

Turin, November 1960. Right through the 1950s and 1960s Renault and Ghia worked together on a variety of highly startling concepts. Under the engineering direction of Fernand Picard, Yves Georges, who ran the Régie's design office, pondered on a revolutionary range-topping vehicle. To optimise accessibility, passenger accommodation and visibility, Renault developed a series of two-box – or more exactly one-box-plus-boot – forward-control prototypes, the engine being at the rear. This architecture created a new interior environment and brought out some interesting relationships between inner room and outer dimensions. Several examples were built and tested in the greatest secrecy. But finally these vehicles, submitted to the scrutiny of the public, were given the thumbs-down, as the extremely forward-set driving position gave a very real impression of being unsafe. So Renault gave up on the idea, but Ghia decided to carry it forward in the form of its own prototypes.

Accordingly a year later the second incarnation of the idea emerged, with the presentation of the Selene Seconda.

From the first cars it retained the concept of the two-box profile and cab-forward design, but the passenger accommodation was differently treated. This was a smaller and more sporting vehicle; its bodywork was painted in a pearlescent white. Aeronautical influences were omnipresent and the design language was no stranger to spaceship cliché: the glazed cockpit and the rear fins very much came from this universe. The Selene Seconda was accompanied by the slogan 'Already Ready for 1970'…

According to Ghia, moving the driving position to the very front and the engine to the very rear reflected the evolution of the aeroplane. However, this grand-touring machine was still more virtual than reality: it wasn't motorised and the coachbuilder contented himself with suggesting that it could accept engines of between 1-litre and 2.5-litre capacity. The car measured 478cm in length, 188cm in width, and 120cm in height, and was built on a 220cm wheelbase. In 1961 the Selene Seconda was displayed again, at the Geneva motor show.

The Selene II marked the end of a series of advanced studies carried out with Renault. The idea was abandoned because the cab-forward driving position made the driver feel unsafe.

ALFA ROMEO 3500 SUPERSPORT (PININ FARINA)

IXG (GHIA)

CHEVROLET CERV I

ALFA ROMEO 3500 SUPERSPORT (PININ FARINA) **Geneva, March 1960**.
Prototype based yet again on the old 8C-3000 CM chassis number 0128. This time the car was a closed coupé with a fully-glazed cockpit, and had lost its scalloped sides, but it retained the *osso di seppia* or cuttlefish-bone profile that would later be taken up on the Duetto. The car was subsequently shown at Frankfurt.

LANCIA LOREYMO (MOTTO)

CHEVROLET CORVETTE XP 700

IXG (GHIA) **Turin, November 1960**. Wedge-shaped aerodynamic dragster, with the driver seated at the very rear, in an extreme reclined position. In June 2002 the IXG was sold by Christie's, as part of the dispersal of the Ghia collection. Length: 480cm. Width: 161cm. Height: 100cm.

CHEVROLET CERV I **Riverside, November 1960**. Experimental single-seater ('Chevrolet Engineering Research Vehicle') conceived by Zora Arkus-Duntov; tubular chassis and aluminium V8. Engine: 4.6-litre V8. Power: 353bhp at 6,200rpm. Length: 436.9cm. Wheelbase: 243.8cm. Maximum speed: 205mph.

LANCIA LOREYMO (MOTTO) **Paris, October 1960**.
Coupé based on the Flaminia and finished in pale chestnut-brown. Designed by Raymond Loewy, and built in Italy by Motto, its styling majored on the aggressiveness of the frontal treatment. An aerofoil channelled air over the rear window. The sole example built survives in the Lancia museum. Engine: Nardi-modified 2,458cc V6. Power: 150bhp. Wheelbase: 252cm.

CHEVROLET CORVETTE XP 700 **New York, April 1960**. Two-seater coupé directly derived from the Corvette, but with a much more aggressive front with four protruding headlamps, cutaway front wheelarches, and a gaping grille. The rear treatment hinted at the '61 Corvette, while the glass hardtop would reappear on the Mako Shark.

CHEVROLET CORVAIR COUPÉ (PININ FARINA)
Paris, October 1960. Coupé based on a shortened Chevrolet Corvair floorpan. The coachwork – in red – developed previously-seen styling themes, in particular the way the flying buttresses of the rear wings flowed into the C-post and defined the rear side window. Variants of the design appeared at the 1962 Paris and 1963 Geneva shows. Wheelbase: 255cm.

PFX (PININ FARINA)

FIAT MARINELLA (FISSORE)

FIAT MARINELLA (FISSORE) **Turin, November 1960**.
Beach car based on the Fiat 600 Multipla, and created in the same spirit as Michelotti's Spiagetta

CHEVROLET CORVAIR COUPÉ (PININ FARINA)

PFX (PININ FARINA) **Turin, November 1960**. Four-door prototype with the unusual configuration of four wheels disposed in a diamond pattern; aerodynamic body with rear fins. Conceived by engineer Alberto Morelli of the Turin Polytechnic, and today preserved in the Pininfarina collection. Engine: Fiat 1,089cc 4-cyl, rear-mounted. Power: 43bhp. Length: 430cm. Width: 171.5cm. Height: 131.5cm. Wheelbase: 207cm plus 97cm.

PLYMOUTH ASSIMETRICA (GHIA)

PLYMOUTH ASSIMETRICA (GHIA) **Turin, October 1961**. Convertible based on the Plymouth Valiant. Following on from 1960's XNR, the Assimetrica initiated Virgil Exner's 'post-modern' style with pronounced winglines emphasising the wheels. The car's name derives from the bulge on the left of the bonnet.

CHEVROLET CORVETTE STING RAY SPIDER

FERGUSON R5 ESTATE (MICHELOTTI)

FERGUSON R5 ESTATE (MICHELOTTI) **London, July 1961**. Four-wheel-drive Ferguson prototype with styling by Giovanni Michelotti. Four-cylinder flat-four designed by Claude Hill. Engine: 2,212cc 4-cyl (dohc). Power: 111bhp at 5,350rpm.

CADILLAC JACQUELINE (PININ FARINA) **Paris, October 1961**. One of a series of Farina Cadillacs, this one (painted eggshell-brown) showcased a further-refined style and cropped wings. In its name it paid homage to Jacqueline Kennedy. Engine: 6,388cc V8. Power: 325bhp. Length: 558cm. Width: 189.5cm. Height: 136cm. Wheelbase: 330.5cm.

CADILLAC JACQUELINE (PININ FARINA)

CHEVROLET CORVETTE STING RAY SPIDER **Chicago, February 1961**. Driven by Dick Thomson in 1959 and 1960, at which stage it was painted red, this sports-racer was transformed into a show-car for 1961; for this role it was re-painted silver-grey. Engine: 4.7-litre V8. Power: 280bhp at 6,200rpm. Maximum speed: 174mph.

PFY (PININ FARINA)

PFY (PININ FARINA) **Turin, October 1961**. In the same spirit as the PFX of 1960, a similar shape was married to Fiat 600D mechanicals, but this time in two-door format and with an orthodox configuration for the four wheels. At first featuring fins, these were later removed.

CHRYSLER TURBOFLITE

CHRYSLER TURBOFLITE **New York, April 1961**. Futuristic vehicle powered by a CR2A gas-turbine. When the doors were opened the cockpit cover pivoted towards the rear. Fully glazed, the cover featured heat-refracting glass. The Turboflite was subsequently shown at the 1961 Paris salon. Power: 140bhp at 39,000rpm.

FORD GYRON **New York, April 1961**. With two seats in tandem, this Alex Tremulis design only had two wheels, balance being assured by a gyroscopic stabiliser. An electronic 'brain' looked after cruise-control, navigation, and other tasks with which the driver would normally be burdened…

ASTON MARTIN JET (BERTONE)

ASTON MARTIN JET (BERTONE) **Geneva, March 1961**. Two-seater coupé based on Aston Martin DB4 GT chassis 0201. One of the first designs by Giorgio Giugiaro, who had joined Bertone in December 1959. Since 1986 the car has been the property of Peter Weidmann, who bough the car from former Aston boss the late Victor Gauntlett. Engine: 6-cyl 3,670cc. Power: 302bhp at 6,000rpm. Length: 436cm. Width: 166cm. Height: 130cm. Wheelbase: 236.2cm.

FORD GYRON

THIS IS AN ICONOCLASTIC MOTOR CAR: IT WAS ONE OF THE RARE FERRARIS CREATED BY BERTONE. FURTHERMORE IT WAS ONE OF THE YOUNG GIORGIO GIUGIARO'S FIRST PROJECTS.

FERRARI 250 GT (BERTONE)

Geneva, March 1962. Ferraris bodied by Bertone are ultra-rare. After having in the main collaborated with Allemano, Touring and Vignale, from 1952 Ferrari began a near-exclusive tie-in with Pininfarina. All the same, in 1960 Bertone created a special 250GT (chassis 1739GT) for a Genoa businessman.

Two years later Giorgio Giugiaro set to in order to design another unique 250GT, this time for Nuccio Bertone himself. It was built on a 250GT swb (240cm wheelbase) with chassis number 3269GT. A gracefully dynamic design, it was the work of a Giugiaro who was only 24 years old but already had the touch of a maestro. It was the creation of a young man, spontaneous and provocative. When he sketched these lines, the stylist had only just been appointed head of design at Bertone, in succession to another great name in the business, Franco Scaglione.

The purists might today reproach the stylist for not having respected the Ferrari image. But this graceful body lacked neither charm nor a sense of reality. The lines were proud, supple, voluptuous. The Bertone Ferrari also emerged as more spacious and more civilised than the production 250GT Berlinetta, styled by Pininfarina. The front, dominated by two wide vaulted air-intakes, meanwhile made reference to the nostrils of the 'Sharknose' F1 Ferrari of the time. The car used the standard mechanicals of the 250GT, such as the 2,953cc V12, developing 270bhp at 7,500rpm.

Shown in marine blue at the 1962 Geneva salon, the Ferrari reappeared at the following Turin show, in November, in a silver-grey. Mexican collector Lorenzo Zambranco bought this exceptional Ferrari in 1980 and gave it a scrupulous restoration by Bob Smith in Texas. Returned to its original colour, it was displayed at the 1997 *Automobiles Classiques* Louis Vuitton concours at Bagatelle.

Magnificently restored in the United States, the Bertone-bodied Ferrari 250GT was one of the great stars of the Automobiles Classiques *Louis Vuitton concours in Paris, at the Parc de Bagatelle, in 1997.*

FORD SEATTLE-ITE XXI

CHEVROLET CORVETTE SHARK

MERCURY PALOMAR

FORD MUSTANG I (TROUTMAN & BARNES)

FORD SEATTLE-ITE XXI Seattle, April 1962. Dream car shown only as a mock-up. Ford's Dearborn styling studio spoke of an interchangeable power source – either electric or (!) nuclear. All the same, who would have thought that the four steered front wheels would resurface on the Tyrell P34 Formula 1 car?

MERCURY PALOMAR
New York, April 1962. Estate car created for the New York World Fair. Modular interior with swivelling front passenger seat and the rearmost bench seat able to face either way. Length: 578cm. Wheelbase: 332.7cm.

FORD COUGAR 406
Dearborn, 1962. Front-engined two-seater with gullwing doors and retractable headlamps. Engine: 6.6-litre V8. Power: 300bhp.

CHEVROLET CORVETTE SHARK New York, April **1962**. Two-seater roadster with glass hardtop, coded XP-755; anticipated the style of the production Corvette Sting Ray of 1963 – in particular in its pronounced waistline crease. Later renamed Mako Shark. Engine: 5,35-litre ZL-1 V8 (supercharged). Power: 456bhp.

ABARTH SPERIMENTALE (VIGNALE)

ABARTH SPERIMENTALE Turin, October 1962. Aerodynamic one-box saloon based on an Abarth-modified Fiat 600D and having an impressive glass area. Rear-mounted 1-litre engine.

FORD MUSTANG I (TROUTMAN & BARNES)
Watkins Glen, October 1962. Shown as a prelude to the US Grand Prix at Watkins Glen, this roadster served as a starting-point for the styling of the Ford GT40; it was built on a Ford Taunus 12M platform, but with a mid-mounted engine (and four-speed gearbox). Engine: 1.5-litre V4. Power: 109bhp at 6,400rpm. Maximum speed: 112mph.

AUSTIN-HEALEY 3000 COUPE (PININFARINA)

AUSTIN-HEALEY 3000 COUPE (PININFARINA)
London, October 1962. Two-plus-two coupé based on the Austin-Healey 3000 MkII. Designed by Pio Manzù, Michael Conrad and Henner Werner of Ulm's Hochschule für Gestaltung, the car won a competition organised by *L'Année Automobile*. Finished in metallic green. Engine: 2,912cc 6-cyl. Power: 132bhp.

FORD COUGAR 406

FERRARI SUPERFAST III (PININFARINA)

FERRARI SUPERFAST III (PININFARINA) **Geneva, March 1962.** After the Superfast of the 1956 Paris salon (chassis 0483SA) and the Superfast II of the 1960 Turin show which prefigured the 400 Superamerica Aerodinamico (chassis 2207SA), the third car to carry the name (chassis 3361SA) developed the theme of its predecessor, in particular with a different glasshouse treatment. Engine: 3,967cc V12. Power: 340bhp. Wheelbase: 242cm.

CHRYSLER TURBINE CAR (GHIA)

PF SIGMA (PININFARINA)

PF SIGMA (PININFARINA) **Turin, October 1963**. Study undertaken at the request of magazine *Quattroruote*. Passive safety features were centred on a strengthened structure, collapsible steering column, sliding doors, and substantial interior padding. A four-seater saloon, there was a single large sliding door either side.

CHRYSLER TURBINE CAR (GHIA) **New York, May 1963**. Continuing its development programme for gas-turbine vehicles, Chrysler produced a series of 50 of these experimental cars. Designed under Elwood P Engel, vice-president in charge of design 1961–72, the cars were built by Ghia. Engine: 130bhp gas-turbine. Length: 512cm. Wheelbase: 280cm.

CHEVROLET TESTUDO (BERTONE)

FORD ALLEGRO

Dearborn, June 1963. Italian-influenced coupé with front-wheel drive, using the Taunus V4 engine. The seats were fixed and the steering wheel and pedals adjustable. This same year Ford also came up with the Mustang II.

FORD COUGAR II

New York, April 1963. Glassfibre-bodied coupé based on Shelby Cobra chassis CSX 2005. Later displayed at the 1966 Brussels Motor Show. Engine: 4,260cc V8. Length: 426cm. Width: 169cm. Height: 121cm. Wheelbase: 229cm.

FORD COUGAR II

CHEVROLET TESTUDO (BERTONE) **Geneva, March 1963**. Futuristic fastback based on the Chevrolet Corvair and thus with rear-mounted engine. The styling, by Giorgio Giugiaro, featured retractable headlamps and a mainly glass hinge-up cockpit cover. Engine: 2,683cc flat-six. Power: 142bhp at 5,200rpm. Length: 430cm. Width: 172cm. Height: 106cm. Wheelbase: 240cm.

CHEVROLET CORVAIR MONZA GT ET SS

FORD ALLEGRO

JAGUAR D-TYPE (MICHELOTTI)

JAGUAR D-TYPE (MICHELOTTI) **Geneva, March 1963**. Coupé styled and built by Giovanni Michelotti on D-Type chassis XKD-513, written off in 1958's Le Mans 24-hours. The racecar-derived proportions gave the body a muscular profile. Engine: 3,442cc 6-cyl. Power: 250bhp. Wheelbase: 229.4cm.

STAR JET (VIGNALE) **Turin, October 1963**. Crowdpuller with no relation to any reality, being half-dragster, half-rocket. That said, the yellow fuselage and the chromed suspension arms, machined by Maserati, were certainly striking.

CHEVROLET CORVAIR MONZA GT ET SS **New York, April 1963**. After the XP-737 Sebring Spyder and the XP-785 Super Spyder, which were closely related to the production Corvair, the fastback GT (as well as the Monza SS roadster shown at the same time) broke new design ground. The cars first appeared as circuit-openers for the 1962 Elkhart Lake 500 race, and were then shown in New York at the same time as the Excalibur Hawk of Brooks Stevens. Engine: 2,375cc flat-six. Power: 140bhp. Length: 420cm. Height: 107cm. Wheelbase: 234cm. Weight: 1,710kg. Maximum speed: 149mph.

STAR JET (VIGNALE)

A MASTERPIECE IN ITS PROPORTIONS, THE CANGURO COUNTS AS ONE OF THE UNCHALLENGED SUCCESSES OF ITALIAN COACHBUILDING. ONCE AGAIN, ALFA ROMEO MECHANICALS WERE THE ALLY OF THE STYLIST.

Paris, October 1964. Having joined Bertone in 1960, Giorgio Giugiaro had by now perfectly mastered his art. For the 1964 Paris salon Nuccio Bertone decided to ready a prototype based on an Alfa Romeo platform. The complicity between the two firms had blossomed in the 1950s, at the time of the fabulous 'BAT' series of cars (1953–55), the birth of the first Giulietta Sprint (1954), and the creation of the 2000 Sportiva

(1956). Thereafter the links between Bertone and Alfa Romeo remained strong, the two collaborating on the Giulietta Sprint Speciale (1957), the 2000 Sprint (1960), and the Giulia Sprint (1963). This time, though, the choice fell on a competition chassis: that of the Giulia Tubolare Zagato – the Zagato styling house being another key partner in the history of Alfa Romeo. The TZ was unveiled at the 1962 Turin show, its claim to fame being its

tubular chassis designed by Edo Mazoni, a trellis of 20–30mm tubes weighing no more than 40kg. This structure led to the name TZ, for 'Tubolare Zagato'.

The running gear owed nothing to the other Giulias either: the suspension was triangulated, there was all-wheel independent suspension, and there were inboard rear brakes. The engine was that of the Giulia SS: a four-cylinder 1,570cc twin-cam developing 112bhp at 6,500rpm. It was

ALFA ROMEO CANGURO (BERTONE)

Using the Alfa Romeo Tubulare chassis, Giorgio Giugiaro succeeded in giving the car more harmonious and less brutal lines. The Canguro had its debut at the Paris Motor Show (left).

around these superb mechanicals that Giorgio Giugiaro wove his talent. On this backcloth the stylist drew up some magnificent lines. The proportions are spot-on, with the nose pert and aggressive, the feline sides gorgeously flowing, a judiciously curved glasshouse, and a dipping beltline. The rear is cut-off, as on the original Giulia TZ, but the design is more refined and less brutal.

At Zagato that excellent stylist Ercole Spada had

come up with efficient, minimalist lines for the TZ, with no purposeless trickery. Bertone added to these an extra dose of grace and elegance while retaining the car's modest dimensions – 390cm length, 160cm width, 106cm height, on a wheelbase of 220cm.

Sold to Germany, then left abandoned for a long time, the Canguro was finally rescued by the Japanese museum Abarth Gallery, which is currently bringing the car back to life.

MERCER COBRA (SIBONA-BASANO)

RENAULT 8 COUPÉ (GHIA)

RENAULT 8 COUPÉ (GHIA) Turin, October 1964. Coupé based on the Renault 8 Gordini. The lines, by Filippo Sapino, picked up on certain themes of pre-war French coachbuilding. Engine: rear-mounted 1,108cc 4-cyl. Power: 90bhp. Wheelbase: 215cm.

MERCER COBRA (SIBONA-BASANO) Paris, October 1964. Roadster built on Shelby Cobra chassis CSX 2451 to illustrate new possible uses for copper and brass. The post-modern styling was the work of Virgil Exner, and the car was built in Turin by Sibona-Basano.

ABARTH 1000 SPYDER SPÉCIALE (PININFARINA)

MERCURY AURORA New York, April 1964. The public discovered this substantial 'lifestyle' estate on Ford's 'Wonder Rotunda' stand at the New York World Fair. An exceptional glass area and clever internal space utilisation characterised this project, which featured a modulable interior with swivelling front passenger seat and the rearmost bench seat having its back to the direction of travel.

MERCURY AURORA

ABARTH 1000 SPYDER SPÉCIALE (PININFARINA) Turin, October 1964. Open sports car with Fiat-derived rear engine. Stripped-down style featuring glass prow incorporating the four headlamps. A coupé version was displayed at the 1965 Frankfurt show. Engine: 982cc 4-cyl. Power: 54bhp. Maximum speed: 100mph.

CHEVROLET RONDINE (PININFARINA)

GENERAL MOTORS RUNABOUT

GENERAL MOTORS FIREBIRD IV New York, April 1964. Final evolution of the Firebird series of cars, shown at New York's World Fair. The car was conceived – supposedly – for rapid journeys on motorways equipped with automatic guidance systems. At the 1964 New York show Chevrolet, meanwhile, displayed its Chevy II Super Nova.

GENERAL MOTORS RUNABOUT New York, April 1964. City car created for women…and shopping. In the same Futurama display at the New York World Fair, General Motors also showed the GMX and the Bison – an articulated lorry powered by two gas-turbines.

MERCEDES-BENZ 230 SL SPÉCIALE (PININFARINA) Paris, October 1964. Coupé based on the Mercedes-Benz 230SL. In doing away with the 'pagoda' roof the car lost much of its personality, despite its pure and well-balanced lines. Engine: 2,281cc 6-cyl. Power: 150bhp. Wheelbase: 240cm.

CHEVROLET RONDINE (PININFARINA) Geneva, March 1964. After being shown in its initial form at the 1963 Paris salon, the Rondine reappeared at Geneva with a panoramic rear window in place of the original flat reverse-rake screen. Engine: 5.4-litre Corvette V8. Wheelbase: 249cm.

MERCEDES-BENZ 230 SL SPÉCIALE (PININFARINA)

GENERAL MOTORS FIREBIRD IV

DINO SPÉCIALE (PININFARINA)

CHEVROLET MAKO SHARK II

DINO SPÉCIALE (PININFARINA) Paris, October

1965. Important design by Aldo Brovarone which would lead to the Dino 206GT. The fastback body (chassis 0840) had numerous innovatory styling details: the concave rear widow, the chopped-off tail, the full-width glass cover for the headlamps, the long side scoops, and the pronounced front wheelarches. The prototype is preserved in the Le Mans motor museum. Engine: 1,987cc V6. Wheelbase: 234cm.

AUTONOVA GT Frankfurt, September 1965. Coupé

based on the NSU Type 110. The design was the work of Pio Manzù and Michael Conrad, who had won the *L'Année Automobile* competition in 1962, and was built in Turin by Sibano-Basano.

AUTONOVA GT

AUTONOVA FAM

AUTONOVA FAM Frankfurt, September 1965.

Four-door one-box design based on Glas mechanicals; designed by Pio Manzù and Michael Conrad. Engine: 1.3-litre 4-cyl. Power: 60bhp. Length: 350cm. Maximum speed: 87mph.

COBRA (GHIA) Turin, October 1965. Two-seater

roadster based on the Shelby Cobra 427 and distinguished by much tauter lines than the original. Engine: 7-litre V8. Power: 431bhp at 4,800rpm. Length: 462cm. Width: 173cm. Height: 133.5cm. Wheelbase: 243.8cm.

COBRA (GHIA)

BUGATTI 101 (GHIA)

BUGATTI 101 (GHIA)

Turin, October 1965. Two-seater roadster based on shortened Bugatti 101C chassis (101506) dating from 1951. The car was purchased by Allen Henderson of New Jersey, then passed to Scott Bailey, and was finally bought – in March 1965 – by Virgil M Exner Inc. The completed vehicle had its début at France Motors, Neuilly-sur-Seine, in October 1965, before being unveiled to the public at the 1965 Turin show. Engine: 3,257cc 8-cyl in-line. Power: 200bhp. Length: 512cm. Width: 173cm. Height: 131cm. Wheelbase: 280cm.

FISSORE ARUANDA

Turin, October 1965. One-box city car created by Ari Antonio da Rocha, winner of a competition to design a town car; sliding doors.

CHEVROLET MAKO SHARK II

New York, April 1965. Coupé which anticipated the next generation of Corvette. Its dark blue coachwork, fading into white metalflake, featured a retractable rear spoiler. At the same show Bertone displayed the Mustang AQ. The Mako Shark went on to be the star of the 1965 Paris show. Engine: 6,489cc 'Porcupine' V8. Power: 425bhp at 6,400rpm. Length: 469cm. Width: 177cm. Height: 117.1cm. Wheelbase: 249cm.

FORD COBRA BORDINAT Dearborn, December

1965. Convertible based on the Shelby Cobra (chassis CSX 2004) and designed under Eugène Bordinat, head of Ford styling 1961–80 – hence the car's name. Ford Fairlane automatic transmission. Engine: 7-litre V8. Length: 428cm. Width: 168cm. Height: 118cm. Wheelbase: 229cm. Weight: 1,110kg.

FORD COBRA BORDINAT

FISSORE ARUANDA

PARTNER TO LAMBORGHINI, CARROZZERIA TOURING WAS NOT GOING TO SURVIVE THE INEVITABLE DISAPPEARANCE OF THE SPECIALIST COACHBUILDER. BUT IT WENT OUT WITH A BANG WITH THE FLYING STAR II.

Final creation of Touring, the Flying Star II developed a theme which has tempted countless stylists: that of a coupé which becomes practical through taking on the false air of a sporting estate.

LAMBORGHINI FLYING STAR II

Turin, November 1966. Founded in 1926 by Felice Bianchi Anderloni, Carrozzeria Touring said its farewells to the motor industry at the Turin show that witnessed the triumph of Giorgio Giugiaro as he unveiled the Maserati Ghibli, De Tomaso Pampero and Mangusta and the Fiat Vanessa under the Ghia banner. For 40 years Touring had made a considerable contribution to the evolution of automotive coachwork, as much from the point of view of aesthetics as in technical matters. Since 1948 the Milan firm had been led by Carlo Felice Bianchi Anderloni, son of the founder, and most of its designs were signed Federico Formenti. At the end of 1966, it was a time to reflect on past glories. For its last-chance salon, Touring prepared two novelties: a Fiat 124 cabriolet and the Lamborghini Flying Star II.

The latter was built on a 400GT 2+2 chassis (number 0904) with the wheelbase shortened to 245cm, giving closer-coupled dimensions – a length of 438cm, a width of 172cm and a height of 120cm. The mechanicals were retained unchanged, in particular the 3,929cc quad-cam V12, developing 320bhp at 6,500rpm and 272lb ft of torque at 4,500rpm.

The style of this Flying Star was original, although its name evoked a celebrated Touring creation of 1931. Its lines respected the great purity of expression which characterised most Touring designs. The sides were smooth and the beltline featured a bevelled upper surface delicately buttressing the full length of the flanks. But it was above all with the car's superstructure that the Flying Star II stood out. The rear was treated like that of a small estate car, with a tailgate taking in the rear window. All the rear was given over to luggage, with the idea of emergency rear seating being abandoned in favour of a strict two-seater configuration.

The dashboard was equally rational, with two large dials facing the driver. After the Turin show, the Flying Star II found a taker in France in the form of Jacques Quoirez, brother of the writer Françoise Sagan. Twenty-one years after its first appearance the Flying Star was again to be seen in Paris, on the occasion of the 1987 Rétromobile show.

FERRARI 365 P TRE POSTI (PININFARINA)

FERRARI 365 P TRE POSTI (PININFARINA) **Paris, October 1966**. This mid-engined GT with three-abreast seating could have rivalled the Lamborghini Miura, but in the end only two were made: one (chassis 8971) for Luigi Chinetti and one with aerodynamic addenda (chassis 8815) for Giovanni Agnelli. Engine: 4,390cc V12. Power: 320bhp. Wheelbase: 260cm.

AMC CAVALIER

PORSCHE 911 ROADSTER (BERTONE)

PORSCHE 911 ROADSTER (BERTONE) **Geneva, March 1966**. Two-seater roadster based on the Porsche 911. At its unveiling there was talk of the car entering limited production for the US market. Engine: 1,991cc flat-six. Power: 130bhp. Wheelbase: 221.1cm.

ALFA ROMEO SCARABEO (OSI) **Paris, October 1966**. Mid-engined 'breadvan' coupé with Guilia GTA power unit and five-speed gearbox. Hinge-up cockpit and set-back driving position. Engine: 1,470cc 4-cyl. Power: 115bhp at 6,000rpm. Length: 372cm. Width: 156cm. Height: 102cm. Wheelbase: 215cm. Weight: 700kg.

AMC CAVALIER

Detroit, June 1966. Attractive four-door saloon with panels (wings, bonnet/boot, bumpers) interchangeable front to rear. Length: 444.5cm. Height: 127cm. Wheelbase: 275cm.

PONTIAC BANSHEE

VAUXHALL XVR

VAUXHALL XVR

Geneva, March 1966. Futuristic gullwing-door coupé of which three were made by Vauxhall's Engineering and Styling Centre in Luton. Designed by Wayne Cherry under the direction of David Jones. Length: 406.4cm. Width: 163.8cm. Height: 102.9cm. Wheelbase: 215.9cm.

DUESENBERG (GHIA)

DUESENBERG (GHIA)

New York, April 1966. Resurrection of the Duesenberg Corporation under M McManis. This imposing Chrysler-powered saloon, dripping with pomposity and ersatz historical detailing, was designed by Virgil Exner and built by Ghia. Engine: 7.2-litre V8. Power: 425bhp. Gearbox: 3-sp automatic. Length: 622cm. Maximum speed: 120mph.

PONTIAC BANSHEE

New York, April 1966. Front-engined 2+2 coupé with accessibility enhanced by the doors sliding to the front and by gullwing hinged roof panels. Engine: 6.9-litre V8. Length: 590cm. Height: 120cm. Wheelbase: 270cm.

AMC AMX II **Detroit, June 1966**. Classically-styled four-seater coupé with retractable headlamps. The rear lights were three-colour: green when the car was moving, orange when it had stopped, and red when it was braking. At the same time AMC showed the Vixen coupé.

AMC AMX II

ALFA ROMEO SCARABEO (OSI)

LANCIA FLAVIA SPORT SPECIAL (ZAGATO)

LANCIA FLAVIA SPORT SPECIAL (ZAGATO) Turin, **November 1967**. One of the last projects of the talented Ercole Spada, who was at Zagato from 1960 until 1969. Very much apparent is his taste for abrupt surface changes and strong styling lines. Engine: 1,800cc flat-four. Power: 100bhp at 5,800rpm. Wheelbase: 248cm.

ALPINE SILVER FOX (OSI)

ALPINE SILVER FOX (OSI)
Turin, November 1967.
Coupé (Cd 0.258) based on the Alpine A110 and taking up the catamaran idea already used by Piero Taruffi on his Bisiluro. Engine: Renault 1,000cc 4-cyl. Length: 413cm. Width: 184cm. Height: 100cm. Wheelbase: 235cm.

CHEVROLET ASTRO I
New York, April 1967.
Extremely low-slung red two-seater coupé dream car, with swing-up cockpit cover and seats rising to aid access. Mid-mounted Corvair flat-six. Engine: 2.9-litre 6-cyl. Length: 448.9cm. Width: 183.5cm. Height: 85.1cm. Wheelbase: 223.5cm.

FORD COMUTA

BMC 1800 AERODINAMICO (PININFARINA)

FORD COMUTA

FORD COMUTA
Dunton, June 1967.
Conceived at Ford's UK research and development centre in Dunton, Essex, this prototype electric city car (range 40 miles) had its public debut in the United States. Length: 203.2cm. Width: 125.3cm. Height: 142.2cm. Wheelbase: 135.9cm. Weight: 540kg. Maximum speed: 25mph.

BMC 1800 AERODINAMICO (PININFARINA) Turin, **November 1967**. Two-box aerodynamic saloon based on the Austin 1800, and which would have a determining influence on the next generation of big saloons (not least the Citroën CX); styling by Leonardo Fioravanti. Pininfarina's other 1967 offerings were the Dino Berlinetta Prototipo Competizione (Frankfurt) and the Fiat Dino Berlinetta (Paris).

CHEVROLET ASTRO I

AMC AMX III SPORTSWAGON New York, **April 1967**. Under the direction of Richard Teague (in office 1964–85), the American Motors styling department yet again distinguished itself with this superb grand-touring estate, whose frontal treatment would be taken up on production models. At the same show Dodge showed the interesting Deora pick-up and Ford the Mustang Mach I.

FORD MACH II

FORD MACH II Chicago, **February 1967**. Two-seater mid-engined coupé with semi-monocoque steel hull and plastic body; Mustang front suspension. Shown again at the 1968 New York show. Engine: 4.7-litre V8. Length: 445cm. Width: 173cm. Height: 120cm. Wheelbase: 272cm. Weight: 1,200kg.

AMC AMX III SPORTSWAGON

LAMBORGHINI MARZAL (BERTONE)

LAMBORGHINI MARZAL (BERTONE) Geneva, **March 1967**. Four-seater coupé anticipating the Lamborghini Espada. The lines, the work of Marcello Gandini, featured fully-glazed gullwing doors and a hexagonal motif used both in the interior and on the exterior. Engine: 1,965cc 6-cyl. Power: 175bhp at 6,800rpm. Length: 445cm. Width: 170cm. Height: 108cm. Wheelbase: 262cm. Weight: 1,310kg. Maximum speed: 118mph.

1968

THE CARABO IS ONE OF THOSE PROJECTS THAT PUSH THE EVOLUTION OF STYLING FORWARD, FAR INTO THE FUTURE, THANKS TO THE MAGIC OF AN UNBRIDLED HAND AT THE PENCIL. THIS PARTICULAR EXERCISE WAS SIGNED MARCELLO GANDINI.

ALFA ROMEO CARABO (BERTONE)

Paris, October 1968. The arrow-shaped prototype that was unveiled at the Porte de Versailles was one of the most captivating in the history of specialist coachbuilding. Adding to the sense of occasion, Nuccio Bertone had come to Paris with his new press and communications chief Gianbeppe Panicco.

Marcello Gandini, recruited by Bertone three years previously, had outlined a wedge-shaped form inspired, perhaps, by the gas-turbine Lotus 56 which had contested the 1968 Indy 500. The volumes were structured by the side gills which gave tension to the monolithic
silhouette with its plane surfaces and pointed prow, while the play of contrasting colours – the green of the body and the orange of the glass – gave an animality to the machine. Fluorescent paint, orange at the front and green at the rear, was intended to convey an element of safety.

The slats covering the engine bay made one think of the scales of a beast, while the pivoting doors opened up like bat's wings, via a hydropneumatic system. The glazing, meanwhile, was by the Belgian company VHR-Glabverbel and was treated to refract the rays of the sun.

The Carabo was based, once again, on the mechanicals of an Alfa Romeo racer, in this instance the Tipo 33 with its V8 engine (1,995cc, developing 230bhp at 9,000rpm and maximum torque of 151.9lb ft at 6,000rpm). Alfa Romeo developed this model specifically for racing, and it was to be available in various versions, including a 3-litre with either eight cylinders or twelve, running from the 33/3 of 1969 to the 33SC 12 which gave Alfa the sports-car world championship in 1977. On the 235cm wheelbase of the 33 the Carabo emerged with a length of 417.6cm, a width of 178.5cm, and a height of 99cm.

The Alfa 33 mechanicals inspired numerous stylists. Marazzi produced a small series of the magnificent 33 Stradale styled by Franco Scaglione. Giorgio Giugiaro put his signature to the Iguana (Turin 1969), while Pininfarina developed three prototypes: the Roadster (Turin 1968), the Prototipo Speciale derived from his Ferrari P5 (Paris 1969), and the Cuneo Spider Speciale (Brussels 1971). Bertone subsequently came up with a second coupé, the Navajo (Geneva 1976).

The Carabo was supposed to be good for 162mph, but since it has been put out to pasture in the Alfa Romeo collection its horses have become somewhat recalcitrant!

With its sharp-edged profile, its wing-like doors and its insect-derived colouring, the Carabo was a stylist's dream-car that emerged perfectly honed.

AMC AMITRON

BIZZARRINI MANTA (ITAL DESIGN) Turin, October 1968. One-box mid-engined GT based on the tubular-chassis Bizzarrini 538; the first creation of Giorgio Giugiaro under his own name, having set up Ital Design with Luciano Bosio, Gino Boaretti and Aldo Mantovani. Engine: Chevrolet V8. Power: 400bhp. Length: 410cm. Width: 185.5cm. Height: 105cm. Wheelbase: 250cm.

CHEVROLET ASTRO II (XP 880)

CHEVROLET ASTRO II (XP 880) New York, March 1968. Mid-engined GT more realistic and more civilised than Astro I. At the same show GM displayed the Asto-Vette, a roadster based on the 1968 Corvette. Engine: 7-litre V8. Power: 390bhp. Length: 450cm. Width: 185cm. Height: 109cm. Wheelbase: 250cm.

FORD TECHNA

ROVER P6BS/LEYLAND EIGHT

ROVER P6BS/LEYLAND EIGHT New York, March 1968. Mid-engined prototype (Cd 0.42) developed by Rover and built at Alvis under the direction of Spen King; transmission designed at Alvis under Mike Dunn and rear De Dion suspension based on that of the Rover P6. Engine: Traco-tuned 3.5-litre V8. Power: 270–320bhp. Weight: 1,067kg.

AMC AMITRON

Detroit 1968. Urban vehicle powered by an electric motor giving a range of 180 miles. American Motors brought the Amitron out again in June 1977 under the name Concept Electron, showing at the same time four new concept cars – Concept I, Concept II, Grand Touring, and an interesting compact van called Concept AM Van.

FORD TECHNA

Dearborn, August 1968. Six-seater coupé with offset propshaft; wide (180cm) sliding doors with an elaborate mechanism, operated by remote control. At the Detroit Auto Show in November Ford displayed the Saturn II. Length: 530cm. Wheelbase: 300cm. Weight: 2,150kg.

SERENISSIMA (GHIA)

FERRARI 250 P5 (PININFARINA)

FERRARI 250 P5 (PININFARINA)

FERRARI 250 P5 (PININFARINA) Geneva, March 1968. Mid-engined GT styled by Leonardo Fioravanti. The scalloped wheelarches, the air vents in the side scoops, the rear end with its strakes and the bank of headlamps behind their glass cover all constitute important motifs. Other 1968 Pininfarina creations were the Fiat Dino Ginevra (Geneva), the Bentley T Coupé (London), the BLMC 1100 Aerodinamica (Turin), the Alfa Romeo 33 Spider (Turin), and the Ferrari P6 (Turin). The Ferrari 250 P5 was reconstructed by Pininfarina in 2000, for the Abarth Gallery.

SERENISSIMA (GHIA) Turin, October 1968. Mid-engined GT designed by Tom Tjaarda. Other than its very pure lines, one of the stylistic motifs is the perforated central pillar evoking the structure underneath. At the same show Fiat displayed the Autobianchi Prototipo (G31) – a mid-engined coupé – and the City-Taxi. Engine: 3-litre V8. Length: 427cm. Width: 183cm. Height: 106cm. Wheelbase: 255cm.

AMC AMX-GT New York, March 1968. Very sculpted coupé representing a stage in the renewal of AMC's image orchestrated by Richard Teague. That same year Chrysler, which wasn't at that time running AMC, showed its Dodge Charger II.

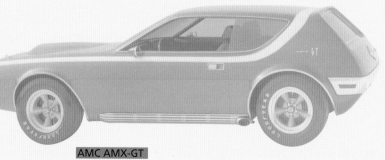

AMC AMX-GT

FORD BERLINER

FERRARI 512 S BERLINETTA SPÉCIALE (PININFARINA)

FERRARI 512 S BERLINETTA SPÉCIALE (PININFARINA) Turin, October 1969.
Mock-up for a GT based on the Ferrari 512S, with wedge-shaped lines by Filippo Sapino; currently on display at the Musée de l'Automobile at Mougins. At Turin Pininfarina also showed the Fiat Teenager, while Bertone displayed the Autobianchi Runabout and a Fiat 128 coupé and Ital Design an Abarth 1600 study. Length: 465cm. Width: 196.5cm. Height: 98.2cm. Wheelbase: 240cm.

AMC AMX/2

FERRARI SIGMA GRAND PRIX (PININFARINA)

FERRARI SIGMA GRAND PRIX (PININFARINA)
Geneva, March 1969. A study for an F1 car with maximum passive safety, evolved in collaboration with Paul Frère and Ernst Fiala; features included a progressively deformable structure and a protected fuel tank. The chassis was from a 1966 F1 Tipo 312 Ferrari – number 0011. Other Pininfarina creations in 1969 were the Abarth 2000 (Brussels), the Alfa Romeo 33 Prototipo Speciale (Paris), and the Fiat 128 Teenager (Turin). Engine: 3-litre V12. Length: 419.5cm. Width: 191cm. Height: 93cm. Wheelbase: 240cm. Weight: 590kg.

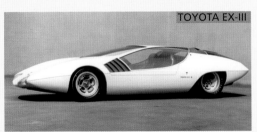

TOYOTA EX-III

FORD BERLINER
Geneva, March 1969. One-box hyper-compact city car designed – very attractively – by Hans Muth. Length: 213cm. Width: 137cm. Height: 137cm.

AMC AMX/2 **Chicago, March 1969**. Mid-engined GT with a sleek glass-fibre body designed under Richard Teague. The same year saw less inspired offerings from Ford and Chrysler: the Ford Super Cobra, the Mercury Super Spoiler, the Chrysler Concept 70X, and the Plymouth Duster I. Engine: V8. Length: 435.6cm. Height: 109.2cm. Wheelbase: 266.7cm.

TOYOTA EX-III **Tokyo, November 1969**. This mid-engined GT was one of the first serious attempts by a Japanese manufacturer to tackle a concept car, and was characterised by an original shape and a clever form for the glasshouse. At the same show Toyota displayed the front-engined EX-I coupé and the EX-II city car, while Isuzu showed its Bellett MX1600.

BRITISH LEYLAND ZANDA (PRESSED STEEL FISHER)

BRITISH LEYLAND ZANDA (PRESSED STEEL FISHER)
London, October 1969. Remarkable styling exercise – a non-runner – conceived by Harris Mann of the Austin-Morris styling department; mid-mounted Maxi 1500cc engine envisaged.

MERCEDES-BENZ CIII

MERCEDES-BENZ CIII **Frankfurt, September 1969**. Experimental GT serving as a test-bed for Wankel rotary-engine technology under licence from NSU. Styled (Cd 0.33) under Karl Wilfert; a second version, more evolved in its lines, was unveiled at the 1970 Geneva show. Engine: mid-mounted three-rotor Wankel. Power: 280bhp at 7,000rpm. Gearbox: ZF five-speed. Length: 423cm. Width: 180cm. Height: 112cm. Wheelbase: 262cm. Weight: 1,100kg. Maximum speed: 168mph.

CHEVROLET ASTRO III
Chicago, March 1969. Completely utopian three-wheeler, windtunnel-evolved and powered by a 317bhp 250-C18 gas-turbine from GM's Allison subsidiary. At the same show General Motors also displayed the Pontiac Cirrus, while a month later it unveiled the 512 city-car prototypes, the three-wheel 511 Commuter, and the small XP-883 concept.

CHEVROLET ASTRO III

CERTAIN CONCEPT CARS BELONG MORE TO THE WORLD OF WORKS OF ART BECAUSE OF THE CREATIVE LIBERTY THAT HAS ANIMATED THEM. THE SCULPTURAL MODULO SHAPED BY PAOLO MARTIN AROUND FERRARI MECHANICALS IS AN ILLUSTRATION OF THIS APPROACH.

Geneva, March 1970. In the same way as Bertone's Carabo, this Pininfarina prototype put itself far beyond the other side of the recurring fashions and tendencies of contemporary coachwork. Stylist Paolo Martin positioned himself quite consciously elsewhere, at the very margin of existing currents of thought and influences, approaching the Modulo project as a veritable mobile sculpture.

Born in 1943, Martin followed a tortuous path

which led him into the most fertile gardens of the mind in Italian coachbuilding. He began his career with Giovanni Michelotti, where he learnt the arts of drawing, modelling and metalworking. Then he spent a few months with Bertone before in 1967 becoming head of styling at Pininfarina. Three years later he put his signature to what was his uncontested masterpiece.

The body of the Modulo was characterised by its two superimposed shells, separated by a waistline

ridge forming a belt around the whole. In essence it is a monolithic single-volume construction, and the machine ressembles an extraordinary spaceship.

The passenger compartment received light in an original way, through the arrival of 'cold light' via a luminescent panel taking up the surface of the roof, a system developed with Galileo of Florence. The entire canopy slid rearwards for access to the interior.

The Modulo used a Ferrari 512S chassis with a wheelbase of 240.5cm, this leading to not

inconsiderable dimensions – a length of 448cm, a width of 204.8cm, and a height of 93.5cm. The engine, mid-mounted, was a quad-cam V12. With a capacity of 4,993cc, it developed 550bhp at 8,000rpm and maximum torque of 369lb ft at 5,500rpm.

The Modulo was unveiled at the 1970 Geneva show, in black. Subsequently repainted in white, it was displayed at numerous international exhibitions: the Osaka Expo in 1970, the 1970 Turin show, the April 1972 New York Auto Show, the May 1972 Auto Expo in Los Angeles, and The World Trade Fair in Vancouver.

In 1976 Paolo Martin regained his independence and went on to produce several further remarkable designs, even if they were less spectacular.

The stylist Paolo Martin let his imagination run riot on the fringes of the plastic arts: the Modulo is one of the most audacious sculptures in the history of automotive design.

CHEVROLET CORVETTE PROTOTYPE (XP 882)

CHEVROLET CORVETTE PROTOTYPE (XP 882) **New York, April 1970**. Built in 1968, but then put on ice by John Z De Lorean, the XP 882 was brought out of store in riposte to Ford's De Tomaso Pantera, the arrival of which also prompted AMC's AMX/3. It was the first car to have a transversely-disposed mid-mounted V8. Length: 443cm. Width: 190cm. Height: 108cm. Wheelbase: 242cm. Weight: 1,177kg.

VW-PORSCHE MURÈNE (HEULIEZ)

VW-PORSCHE MURÈNE (HEULIEZ) **Paris, October 1970**. Coupé based on the VW-Porsche 914/6 and styled by Jacques Cooper, designer of the TGV high-speed train for Alsthom. The Murène provided the first evidence of the styling abilities of French coach-builder Heuliez. Engine: 1,991cc flat-six. Power: 110bhp at 5,800rpm. Wheelbase: 245cm.

TOYOTA EX-7

TOYOTA EX-7 **Tokyo, November 1970**. Mid-engined GT based on the Toyota 7 racer. Relative to other Japanese creations of the time, this was one of the less baroque; power came from a 5-litre V8. Also at Tokyo was Toyota's three-wheel Commuter city car.

VAUXHALL SRV
London, October 1970. Ultra-streamlined four-door four-seater saloon with mid-mounted transverse engine; fixed seats and adjustable pedals. Length: 508cm. Width: 194cm. Height: 105cm. Wheelbase: 267cm.

NISSAN 126X

NISSAN 126X **Tokyo, November 1970**. Four-seater mid-engined GT. The cockpit hinged towards the front, the styling was brutally geometric, and lights shone through the vents in the bonnet. At Tokyo Nissan also showed the front-wheel-drive 270X and the 315 XA small car. Engine: 3-litre 6-cyl. Power: 180bhp.

MAZDA RX-500 **Tokyo, November 1970**. Mazda decided in its turn to showcase its know-how with this GT, premièred at Hiroshima in February in celebration of the company's 50th anniversary; power came from a mid-mounted rotary. At Tokyo Mazda also showed the EX 005 concept car, a four-seater one-box electric city car.

LANCIA STRATOS (BERTONE)

LANCIA STRATOS (BERTONE) **Turin, October 1970**. Futuristic mid-engined GT characterised by its one-box body, wedge profile and limited glass area; access was via the windscreen. The power unit was the 1.6-litre V4 from the Fulvia HF. At Geneva, Bertone had shown the BMW Garmisch. Length: 385cm. Width: 187cm. Height: 84cm. Wheelbase: 222cm.

VW-PORSCHE TAPIRO (ITAL DESIGN)

VW-PORSCHE TAPIRO (ITAL DESIGN) **Turin, October 1970**. Mid-engined GT based on the VW-Porsche 914/6, with an engine tuned by Bonomelli. Other notable concept cars at Turin included Zagato's Oldsmobile NART and Ghia's De Tomaso Vignale. Engine: 2.4-litre flat-six. Power: 220bhp at 7,200rpm. Length: 406cm. Width: 176cm. Height: 111cm. Wheelbase: 245cm.

MAZDA RX-500

VAUXHALL SRV

FORD GT 70 (GHIA)

ALFA ROMEO 33 SPIDER SPECIALE (PININFARINA) Brussels, January 1971. Final car of Pininfarina's Alfa Romeo 33 trilogy, this time with an extreme wedge shape; the same year Pininfarina also displayed his lamentably ungainly NSU Ro80 saloon. Engine: quad-cam 1,995cc V8. Power: 230bhp at 8,800rpm. Wheelbase: 235cm.

FORD GT 70 (GHIA)
Turin, November 1971. Mid-engined GT based on Ford's GT70 would-be rally-car; styled by Filippo Sapino, head of Ford's Turin design studio. At the same show Ghia also displayed the De Tomaso 1600, a follow-up to the Zonda shown at Geneva.

DE TOMASO ZONDA (GHIA)

DE TOMASO ZONDA (GHIA) Geneva, March 1970. Conventional front-engined coupé which would have made a welcome stablemate for the Mangusta; Ford mechanicals and automatic transmission. Engine: 5,563cc V8. Power: 350bhp at 6,000rpm. Length: 451cm. Width: 188cm. Height: 115cm. Wheelbase: 255cm. Weight: 1,550kg.

ALFA ROMEO 33 SPIDER SPECIALE (PININFARINA)

MATRA LASER (MICHELOTTI)

NISSAN 216 X Tokyo, November 1971. Two-seater coupé with an emphasis on passive safety; four-cylinder 2-litre mid-mounted engine, set transversely. Other concept cars displayed at Tokyo included the Daihatsu BCX, the Toyota RV-1, and the Isuzu Sports Wagon.

NISSAN 216 X

FERRARI 3X (ZAGATO)
Turin, November 1971. Successor to Ercole Spada, Giuseppe Mittino produced his first design for Zagato in response to an order from Luigi Chinetti, the US Ferrari importer; the sharp-edged lines were certainly true to the spirit of Zagato style. Engine: 2,953cc V12. Power: 250bhp at 7,500rpm.

MATRA LASER (MICHELOTTI) Geneva, March 1971. Mid-engined coupé inspired by the Matra 530, its lines overburdened by chrome decoration; gullwing doors. Engine: 2,550cc (Ford 26M) V6. Power: 125bhp at 5,300rpm. Wheelbase: 256cm.

FERRARI 3X (ZAGATO)

ALFA ROMEO CAIMANO (ITAL DESIGN)

FORD MUSTANG MILANO

ALFA ROMEO CAIMANO (ITAL DESIGN) Turin, November 1971. Angular-lined Alfasud-based coupé reviving the idea of the hinged cockpit cover seen on the Testudo 4. Engine: 1,186cc flat-four. Length: 392cm. Width: 165cm. Height: 109cm. Wheelbase: 225cm.

FORD MUSTANG MILANO Chicago, April 1971. Two-seater coupé of Italian inspiration, with an elegance somewhat surprising in an American styling world where such refinement was often lacking. Other US concept cars in 1971 included Ford's Tridon and Maverick Estate Coupé (New York), and the Jeep XJ001 and Dodge Diamante (Chicago).

WITH SAFETY AT LAST BECOMING A PRIORITY IMPOSED ON ALL CAR-MAKERS, BMW RESPONDED, WITH PAUL BRACQ, BY UNVEILING A MACHINE RETAINING DRIVING PLEASURE AND EFFICIENCY.

Paris, October 1972. Born in Bordeaux in 1933, Paul Bracq studied at the Ecole Boulle and cut his teeth working with stylist Philippe Charbonneaux. Having gone to Germany for his national service, Paul Bracq settled there. From 1957 until 1966 he forged his art in the Mercedes-Benz advanced-styling studio; in the same period he met Alice, his most fervent admirer and his future wife. After a brief spell in France at sub-contract coachbuilder, Brissonneau & Lotz, Bracq re-crossed the Rhine in 1969, as director of styling for BMW.

In this position he managed to convince the board of BMW to come up with a prototype giving expression to the technological progress made by the firm. Two themes were developed:

BMW TURBO (MICHELOTTI)

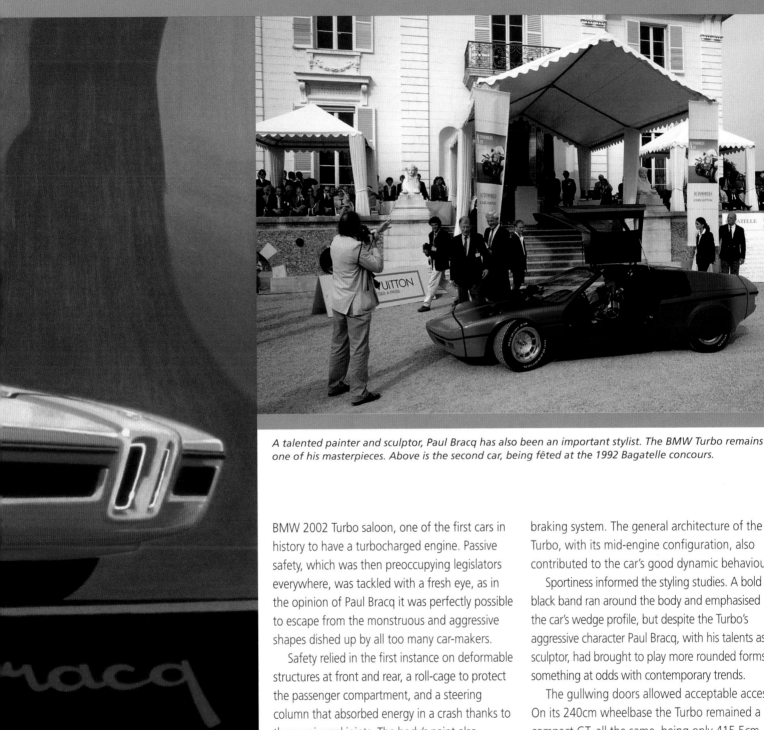

A talented painter and sculptor, Paul Bracq has also been an important stylist. The BMW Turbo remains one of his masterpieces. Above is the second car, being fêted at the 1992 Bagatelle concours.

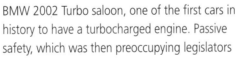

forced induction and safety. The classic 1,990cc four-cylinder in-line engine was boosted with a turbocharger: according to boost pressure, output varied from 200bhp to 280bhp, with a maximum torque of 172.2lb ft. From 1973 BMW sold a

BMW 2002 Turbo saloon, one of the first cars in history to have a turbocharged engine. Passive safety, which was then preoccupying legislators everywhere, was tackled with a fresh eye, as in the opinion of Paul Bracq it was perfectly possible to escape from the monstruous and aggressive shapes dished up by all too many car-makers.

Safety relied in the first instance on deformable structures at front and rear, a roll-cage to protect the passenger compartment, and a steering column that absorbed energy in a crash thanks to three universal joints. The body's paint also contributed to safety, being in a chameleon fluorescent orange fading to solid red. The nose and the tail were robust bumper-shields in composites, to absorb energy in an accident.

Active safety, naturally enough, was also taken into account as a primary concern by BMW, most notably in the installation of an ABS anti-lock

braking system. The general architecture of the Turbo, with its mid-engine configuration, also contributed to the car's good dynamic behaviour.

Sportiness informed the styling studies. A bold black band ran around the body and emphasised the car's wedge profile, but despite the Turbo's aggressive character Paul Bracq, with his talents as a sculptor, had brought to play more rounded forms, something at odds with contemporary trends.

The gullwing doors allowed acceptable access. On its 240cm wheelbase the Turbo remained a compact GT, all the same, being only 415.5cm long, with a width of 188cm and a height of 110cm; it weighed 980kg, and was shod with 4.75/11.2 x 14in tyres.

A second Turbo was built, differing from the first in its rear wheelspats and its paintwork, which faded from orange to brown. Both cars were built by Michelotti, in Turin.

MASERATI BOOMERANG (ITAL DESIGN)

CITROËN CAMARGUE (BERTONE)

MASERATI BOOMERANG (ITAL DESIGN) **Geneva, March 1972**. Sharply wedge-shaped mid-engined GT based on the Maserati Bora. Displayed as a mock-up at the 1971 Turin show but motorised for the 1972 Geneva salon. Engine: 4.7-litre V8. Power: 310bhp at 6,000rpm. Length: 434.2cm. Width: 186cm. Height: 107cm. Wheelbase: 260cm.

CITROËN CAMARGUE (BERTONE) **Geneva, March 1972**. Based on the Citroën GS, this 2+2 coupé had an original rear-end treatment and a pioneering configuration clearly separating the glasshouse from the body's infrastructure. The stark style was the work of Marcello Gandini. Length: 411.5cm. Width: 168cm. Height: 115cm.

ASTON MARTIN SOTHEBY SPECIAL (OGLE) **Montreal, January 1972**. Coupé based on the Aston Martin DBS V8, to the order of tobacco company WD and HO Wills. The contrived coachwork (marine blue with green velours trim) was the work of Ogle, the British independent design house run by Tom Karen. Engine: 5,340cc. Wheelbase: 261cm.

FIAT X1/23

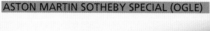

ASTON MARTIN SOTHEBY SPECIAL (OGLE)

TOYOTA RV-2

FIAT X1/23 **Turin, November 1972**. Minimalist city car designed under Gian Paolo Boano, head of Fiat styling from 1959 until 1986. At the same show Lombardi displayed the FL-1 and Zagato its Fiat Aster. Length: 264.2cm. Width: 151cm. Height: 134cm.

TOYOTA RV-2 **Tokyo, November 1972**. Hybrid taking on coupé format for everyday use but transforming into a leisure vehicle for weekends and holidays: the rear of the body extended to become a living area. The RV-2 came to Paris for the 1973 show. At Tokyo in 1972 Toyota also showed the Town Spider small car.

MERCEDES-BENZ ESF 13

MERCEDES-BENZ ESF 13 **Dulles, May 1972**. At the Transpo 72 exhibition in Washington, Mercedes-Benz unveiled the third phase of its ESF programme, making great play of the passive safety offered by the ESF 13's reinforced structure and external protective measures. The programme ultimately comprised five stages: ESF 03 (May 1971), ESF 05 (October 1971), ESF 13 (May 1972), ESF 22 (March 1973), and ESF 024 (June 1974).

ALFA ROMEO ALFETTA SPIDER (PININFARINA)

PEUGEOT TAXI H4 (HEULIEZ)

ALFA ROMEO ALFETTA SPIDER (PININFARINA) **Turin, November 1972**. Targa-top two-seater coupé based on the Alfetta. Beyond its concave sides and its obtrusive bumpers there wasn't much character to the car. Engine: 1,779cc 4-cyl. Power: 122bhp at 5,500rpm.

PEUGEOT TAXI H4 (HEULIEZ) **Paris, October 1972**. Brilliant and forward-looking proposal for a compact one-box taxi, based on the Peugeot 204; designed by Yves Dubernard, who had joined Heuliez in 1971. Intended to be available with different body styles, such as a pick-up and a van. Length: 370cm. Width: 168cm. Height: 126cm. Wheelbase: 253cm.

DAIHATSU BCX-III

NSU TRAPÈZE (BERTONE)

Paris, October 1973. Coupé based on NSU Ro80, and whose four seats were arranged so as to give the maximum room possible within a minimum length: the two front seats were close together, with the two rear seats set outboard. Engine: 497.5cc twin-rotor. Power: 115bhp at 5,500rpm. Width: 183cm.

NSU TRAPÈZE (BERTONE)

CHEVROLET CORVETTE BIROTOR

DAIHATSU BCX-III

Tokyo, November 1973. A forgotten early attempt at a one-box Espace-like approach to the estate car. Access to the rear was by a large sliding door. Other concept cars presented at Tokyo included Toyota's EV-2 and F101.

CHEVROLET XP 898

Chicago, February 1973. Conventional if elegant coupé which retained the classical front-engine configuration, using the Chevrolet Vega 2.3-litre four-cylinder engine; the body was glass-fibre.

CHEVROLET XP 898

CHEVROLET CORVETTE BIROTOR **Frankfurt, September 1973.** Project for a GT (XP 987 GT) designed by Clare MacKichan under Bill Mitchell; built by Pininfarina. Engine: 4.4-litre twin-rotor Wankel. Transmission: 3-sp automatic. Length: 419cm. Width: 166.5cm. Height: 110cm. Wheelbase: 229cm. Weight: 1180kg.

AUTOBIANCHI A112 GIOVANNI (PININFARINA)

Geneva, March 1973. Stripped-out economy coupé with retractable roof panel, intended for the youth market. At the same show Michelotti displayed the Fiat Pulsar, Ghia the Mustela II and Frua the Citroën SMS. Engine: 982cc 4-cyl. Power: 58bhp at 6,000rpm. Length: 332cm. Width: 154cm. Height: 125cm. Wheelbase: 203cm. Maximum speed: 90mph.

JAGUAR XJ-12 PF (PININFARINA)

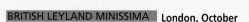

AUTOBIANCHI A112 GIOVANNI (PININFARINA)

JAGUAR XJ-12 PF (PININFARINA) **Paris, October 1973.** While all the same creating an elegant *grande routière*, Pininfarina didn't manage to capture the feline grace of the original XJ-12. Engine: 5,443cc V12. Power: 253bhp at 6,000rpm. Wheelbase: 286.5cm.

DEALER TEAM VAUXHALL

BRITISH LEYLAND MINISSIMA

CHEVROLET CORVETTE 4-ROTOR

BRITISH LEYLAND MINISSIMA **London, October 1973.** City car prototype designed by William Towns; not to be confused with the Mini Electric Car shown by BL in November the same year. Engine: 848cc 4-cyl. Length: 375cm.

CHEVROLET CORVETTE 4-ROTOR **Chicago, February 1973.** Wonderful rotary-powered GT designed by Vinnie Kay and Jerry Palmer; also shown at Paris in October. Engine: 4-rotor Wankel. Power: 350bhp at 7,000rpm. Length: 478.8cm. Width: 181.9cm. Height: 107.9cm. Wheelbase: 342.6cm. Weight: 1,440kg.

THE BRAVO HAD ALL THE ATTRIBUTES OF A FORMIDABLE PRODUCTION GT. BUT AFTER THE RETIREMENT OF FERRUCIO LAMBORGHINI IN 1974, THERE WAS NO QUESTION OF PUTTING IT INTO PRODUCTION, EVEN IN SMALL NUMBERS.

Turin, October 1974. At the same time as the Lamborghini Uracco was on display at the Turin show, in P200 and P300 versions, Bertone unveiled a styling study that could have constituted the replacement for these cars. As with the Miura, the Marzal and the Countach, the Bravo ('Study 114' in Lamborghini-speak) was the fruit of a close collaboration between Bertone and Lamborghini. Like these cars, it wasn't a simple

'special body' but a true prototype whose mechanical basis was totally original.

In particular, one of the decisive changes to the architecture, in comparison to the Uracco, was in the position of the engine, which was set transversely, and not longitudinally. It was still an oversquare V8, of course, of 2,996cc and developing 300bhp, with maximum torque of 235lb ft at 4,000rpm. But turning the engine around allowed the wheelbase to

be reduced to 225cm, making the Bravo an agile and easy-to-handle vehicle. Its length was 373.5cm, with a width of 188cm and a height of 103.5cm. Weight was pared to 1,085kg, and the car was shod with 195/50 VR15 tyres at the front and wider 275/40 VR15s at the rear.

One can't help but consider the Bravo in the same breath as the Stratos, of similar size and designed, as was the Lamborghini, by Marcello

LAMBORGHINI BRAVO (BERTONE)

The sharp edges, the improbably-shaped wheelarches, the shutlines of the glazing and the details of the ornamentation all belong to the design vocabulary of Marcello Gandini.

Gandini. As for its bigger Gandini sister, the Countach, the Bravo, despite its sharp-edged lines, doesn't have that car's violent impact: thanks to its tighter proportions and softer volumes, the Bravo is altogether more graceful. As customary with Bertone, the glazing played a key role in the car's aesthetics, as did the symmetry in its ornamentation – the same multiple air vents in a grid were to be found on both the front and rear. The dashboard used a new material, Alcantara – a synthetic suede which was to become highly popular.

'Bravo' is the name given, in a bullfight, to the bull with the most fight. That said, the Bravo never locked horns. After having covered some 43,500 miles and proved that it was good for 169mph, the prototype joined the Bertone museum.

The Bravo project would be one of the last at Lamborghini to be steered by technical director, Paolo Stanzani before he left Sant'Agata in 1975.

MASERATI COUPÉ (ITAL DESIGN)

ABARTH 2000 SE 027 (PININFARINA)

ABARTH 2000 SE 027 (PININFARINA) Geneva, **March 1974.** Twenty years after the Ferrari 375 Plus, Pininfarina again demonstrated his know-how in the matter of competition machinery, this mid-engined concept having been carefully shaped in the windtunnel. Engine: 1,946cc 4-cyl. Power: 250bhp. Wheelbase: 208.5cm.

LANCIA MIZAR (MICHELOTTI)

MASERATI COUPÉ (ITAL DESIGN) Turin, October **1974.** Strictly conventional 2+2 coupé following on from the Maserati Indy, and conceived with a view to the car's future commercialisation. Engine: 4,931cc V8. Power: 320bhp at 5,500rpm. Length: 472cm. Width: 187cm. Height: 123cm. Wheelbase: 264cm.

LANCIA MIZAR (MICHELOTTI) Geneva, **March 1974.** Saloon based on the Lancia Beta. The four gullwing doors and the retractable headlamps were unusual complexities for a family car. At the front Michelotti used a radiator grille evoking that of the Aurelia. At the same show he also displayed the LEM, an electric town car with four wheels in diamond pattern.

FERRARI STUDIO CR25 (PININFARINA)

FERRARI STUDIO CR25 (PININFARINA) Turin, **October 1974.** Aerodynamic study (Cd 0.256) undertaken to celebrate Pininfarina's construction of a new windtunnel; designed by Aldo Brovarone. Length: 480cm. Width: 192cm. Height: 118cm. Wheelbase: 270cm.

MASERATI MEDICI (ITAL DESIGN)

MASERATI MEDICI (ITAL DESIGN) Turin, October, **1974.** Prestige saloon based on the Maserati *Quattroporte*; the two front seats were clearly separated from the four *vis-à-vis* rear seats. An evolution of the design was shown at Paris in 1976. Engine: 4,930cc V8. Length: 522cm. Width: 186cm. Height: 137cm. Wheelbase: 310cm.

FORD COINS (GHIA) **Geneva, March 1974.** Exactly a year after the announcement of Ghia's takeover by Ford (on 14 March 1973), Ghia showed this wedge-shaped prototype with three-abreast seating, central driving position and access via a rear hatch. Not to mention the spoiler at the top of the windscreen…

FORD COINS (GHIA)

AUDI COUPÉ (FRUA)

AUDI COUPÉ (FRUA) Geneva, **March 1974.** Mid-engined GT with Audi 100 power unit, created by one of the great second-rankers of Italian coachbuilding, the Studio Tecnico Pietro Frua set up in 1959 by the independent stylist of the same name. Engine: 1,871cc 4-cyl. Power: 127bhp.

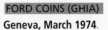

RENAULT BRV

RENAULT BRV London, **June 1974.** Safety prototype in the shape of an R16-sized five-door saloon, shown at the Transport and Road Research Laboratory 'Vehicles and Safety' exhibition. The car was based on the work carried out by Dr Claude Tarrière (of the Laboratory of Physiology and Biomechanics) as part of a link-up between Peugeot and Renault.

TOYOTA MP-1

OPEL GT-2 (MICHELOTTI)

TOYOTA MP-1 Tokyo, November 1975. Important Crown-based prototype which anticipated the first one-box MPVs such as the Nissan Prairie (1982) and the Plymouth Voyager (1983): tall passenger compartment, fallaway bonnet, sliding rear doors, modular interior, wheelchair access. Designed by Ikeda. Also on display at Tokyo was Nissan's AD-1.

OPEL GT-2 (MICHELOTTI) Paris, October 1975. Sliding-door front-engined 2+2 coupé designed by Jean-François Venet under the direction of Henry C Haga; built by Michelotti. Engine: 1,897cc 4-cyl. Power: 105bhp at 5,400rpm. Maximum speed: 120mph.

FORD FLASHBACK

FORD FLASHBACK New York, April 1975. Bizarre two-seater coupé with a 'retro' flavour thanks to its squared-off vertical grille. The compact passenger compartment was at odds with the long bonnet.

ALFA ROMEO EAGLE (PININFARINA)

ALFA ROMEO EAGLE (PININFARINA) Paris, October 1975. Cabriolet with integral roll-bar, styled by Aldo Brovarone and based on the Alfetta GT. This ungainly creation bears witness to the paucity of good design in these crisis years. Engine: 1,779cc 4-cyl. Power: 122bhp at 5,500rpm.

FIAT VISITORS BUS (BERTONE)

NSU Ro80 (GMARMEIER) Geneva, March 1975. Angular coupé with wide gullwing doors, based on the NSU Ro80. Engine: 497.5cc two-rotor Wankel. Power: 115bhp at 5,500rpm.

NSU Ro80 (GMARMEIER)

FIAT VISITORS BUS (BERTONE) Turin, November 1975. One-box minibus intended for the transport of visitors to the Bertone works. Based on the Fiat 850 Familiare.

FIAT 126 CITTÀ (MICHELOTTI)

SBARRO STASH PIERRE CARDIN

FIAT 126 CITTÀ (MICHELOTTI) Geneva, March 1975. One-box town car based on the Fiat 126. Engine: 594cc 2-cyl. Power: 23bhp at 4,800rpm.

SBARRO STASH PIERRE CARDIN Paris, October 1975. Mid-engined coupé whose interior and exterior decoration were the work of Pierre Cardin. Engine: 1,807cc 4-cyl. Power: 147bhp at 5,900rpm. Wheelbase: 265cm. Weight: 1,080kg. Maximum speed: 130mph.

Austérité oblige, designers were becoming more pragmatic. Notwithstanding this, Ital design shone on the occasion of a competition on the theme of the taxi run by the New York Museum of Modern Art.

ALFA ROMEO TAXI (ITAL DESIGN)

New York, June 1976. After the organisation of the 'Taxi Project' competition at New York's Museum of Modern Art it was possible to discern a real grappling of consciences concerning the problems engendered by the use of cars in town. The exhibition was set up at the instigation of MOMA's department of design and architecture, and ran from 15 June to 7 September 1976 under the title 'Taxi Project: Realistic Solutions for Today'.

The presence of the car in town was becoming more and more undesirable. In certain cities the levels of pollution, the traffic saturation and the lack of parking spaces had reached a dramatic level.

In spite of the undeniable advantages the automobile had brought to society, the whole question of the car was unresolved, because it wasn't limited to dealing with the effects of pollution. The choking of cities caused by the increasing number of vehicles on the road constituted another crucial issue. Personal transport in town needed an in-depth reform of its basic structures. Any limitation in the use of private cars presupposed the setting-up of a system of public transport that would be beyond reproach. Hence the attractive solution of the taxi.

Five teams of designers were invited to New York: three from Europe – Ital Design, Volkswagen and Volvo – and two from America – AMF (American Machine and Foundry Inc) and SPS (Steam Power Systems). Volkswagen contented itself with a re-arranged Kombi, while Volvo and Ital Design came up with more innovative solutions which called into question the conventional proportions of the private motor-car. But beyond its conceptual cleverness the Swedish solution was singularly lacking in style...

At Ital Design, in contrast, Giorgio Giugiaro treated the subject with his habitual panache. The vehicle managed to avoid being ungainly despite its unfortunate proportions – a length of 406cm, a width of 174cm and a height of 178cm, the whole built on a 230cm wheelbase. The base came from a van, the Alfa Romeo F12, propelled by a four-cylinder 2-litre engine developing 150bhp.

The Ital Design solution offered an exceptional ratio of accommodation to overall size. Compact, the taxi had a surface area of only 6.98 square metres, against nearly 10 square metres for a conventional American car. The sliding rear doors gave access to a highly functional rear compartment which could accommodate five passengers facing each other.

After its presentation in New York, the Taxi was shown as part of the travelling 'Carrozzeria Italiana' exhibition, in Turin in 1978, Moscow in 1979 and Pasadena in 1981. Thereafter it became part of the Museo Storico Alfa Romeo in Arese.

Before the fashion for one-box designs established itself once and for all, Giorgio Giugiaro explored the benefits of a tall and spacious vehicle, on the occasion of a New York design competition on the theme of taxis.

COLANI L'AIGLON

BMW ASSO DI QUADRI (ITAL DESIGN)

BMW ASSO DI QUADRI (ITAL DESIGN) Turin, **November 1976**. Sensibly-proportioned coupé based on the BMW 320, built to order for Karmann. Engine: 1,990cc 4-cyl. Power: 109bhp at 6,000rpm. Length: 423.5cm. Width: 165cm. Height: 124cm. Wheelbase: 265.3cm.

ALFA ROMEO NAVAJO (BERTONE)

FORD CORRIDA (GHIA)

Turin, November 1976. Gullwing-door coupé inspired by the Fiesta and characterised by its angular lines. The boot was extendable thanks to its drawer-like way of opening. At Geneva Ghia had shown its Urban Car and Mustang III design studies. Engine: 1,117cc 4-cyl. Length: 385.5cm. Width: 164.5cm. Height: 121.2cm. Wheelbase: 28.5cm.

FORD CORRIDA (GHIA)

FORD PRIMA (GHIA)

New York, April 1976. Modular fwd vehicle which could be converted into a two-seat coupé, three-door saloon or an estate car, thanks to different steel hardtops that could be fitted to the base pick-up. The Prima was also shown at Turin, and its concept was to be exploited by Nissan with its series-production EXA model. Length: 399cm. Width: 154cm. Height: 135cm. Wheelbase: 229cm.

PONTIAC BANSHEE II

FORD PRIMA (GHIA)

COLANI L'AIGLON

Geneva, March 1976. Neo-classic roadster, as over-the-top as might be expected from creator Luigi Colani. Roughly 7m (23ft) long, and powered by a 240bhp 5.4-litre Chevrolet V8, with Rolls-Royce front suspension and an Opel Diplomat rear. Named after the king of Rome, son of Napoleon Bonaparte…

PONTIAC BANSHEE II

Paris, October 1976. Four-seater coupé (red with a red interior) incorporating research into passive safety, most evident in the prominent composite bumpers.

ALFA ROMEO NAVAJO (BERTONE)

Geneva, March 1976. Yet another GT inspired by the Tipo 33; but this time the result was less convincing than the Carabo. The rear wing, the bigger glasshouse and the broader beltline all contributed to the heaviness of the design. Engine: 1,997cc V8. Power: 230bhp at 9,000rpm. Wheelbase: 235cm.

FERRARI RAINBOW (BERTONE)

FERRARI RAINBOW (BERTONE)

Turin, November 1976. Mid-engined coupé with retractable hardtop, based on a shortened Dino 308 GT4. The lines laid down by Marcello Gandini were angular in the extreme. Engine: 2,927cc V8. Power: 240bhp. Wheelbase: 245cm.

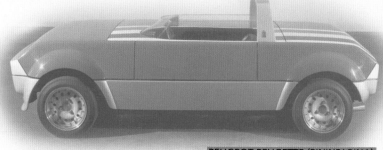

PEUGEOT PEUGETTE (PININFARINA)

PEUGEOT PEUGETTE (PININFARINA) Turin, **November 1976**. Roadster (in orange) based on the Peugeot 104ZS; designed by Diego Ottina and symmetrical front to rear. Engine: 1,124cc 4-cyl. Power: 66bhp at 6,200rpm. Length: 333cm. Width: 153.5cm. Height: 114cm. Wheelbase: 222cm. Maximum speed: 96mph.

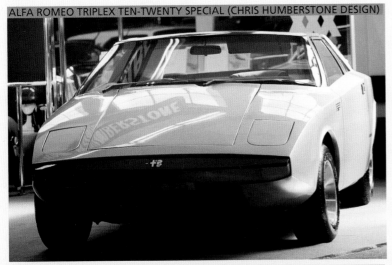

ALFA ROMEO TRIPLEX TEN-TWENTY SPECIAL (CHRIS HUMBERSTONE DESIGN)

ALFA ROMEO TRIPLEX TEN-TWENTY SPECIAL (CHRIS HUMBERSTONE DESIGN)
Geneva, March 1977. Already seen at the 1976 London Motor Show, this prototype ordered by Triplex could accommodate six people on three rows of two seats, those at the front and rear being close together and those in the middle being positioned as far outboard as possible.

PONTIAC TYPE K

Geneva, March 1977. Based on the Pontiac Firebird Trans-Am, this was one of countless attempts to make an estate out of a coupé, along the lines of Pininfarina's Peugeot Riviera (Paris 1971). Designed by Jerry Brockstein for David Holls; built by Pininfarina. The side windows open gullwing-style.

PONTIAC TYPE K

JAGUAR ASCOT (BERTONE)

TOYOTA ABEV Tokyo, **November 1977**. This ungainly coupé was supposed to demonstrate Toyota's mastery of aluminium – hence 'ABEV', short for 'Aluminium Body Experimental Vehicle'. Toyota's other concept cars shown at Tokyo were the F110 saloon and the Cal-1 pick-up, the latter created by Calty, Toyota's studio in California; Nissan, meanwhile, displayed its AD-2.

MATRA MS15 Vélizy, **1977**. Compact sporting saloon conceived by Joël Le Charpy and designed by Antoine Volanis, under the direction of Philippe Guédon. The passenger compartment featured four separate seats. Based on the fwd powerpack (1.6-litre, 5-sp gearbox) of the Simca Horizon. Length: 335cm.

MATRA MS15

FORD MEGASTAR (GHIA)
Geneva, March 1977. Saloon based on the Granada. The ovoid side treatment encompassed a generous glass area. A Megastar II would appear at the 1978 Geneva show. Length: 440cm. Width: 186.4cm. Height: 124.5cm.

FORD MEGASTAR (GHIA)

JAGUAR ASCOT (BERTONE) Geneva, March 1977. Four-seater coupé based on shortened XJ-S platform. Marcello Gandini's style remained as sharp-lined as ever. Engine: 5,343cc V12. Power: 289bhp at 5,500rpm. Wheelbase: 239cm.

TOYOTA ABEV

CHEVROLET AEROVETTE

CHEVROLET AEROVETTE Warren, **1977**. Two-seater mid-engined GT, developed from 1973's Corvette 4-Rotor but now with conventional V8 power.

ALPINE A110 (MEYRIGNAC)

ALPINE A110 (MEYRIGNAC) Geneva, March 1977. Wedge-shaped coupé based on the rear-engined Alpine A110, its grp body the work of Denis Meyrignac. Engine: 1,647cc Renault 4-cyl. Power: 95bhp. Length: 382cm. Width: 172cm. Height: 107cm. Wheelbase: 210cm. Weight: 800kg.

AFTER THE FUEL CRISIS, DESIGNERS FOCUSED THEIR ATTENTION ON LOWERING PETROL CONSUMPTION. ON THIS SCORE THE IDEAL FORM AS DEFINED BY PININFARINA WOULD SERVE AS A POINT OF REFERENCE.

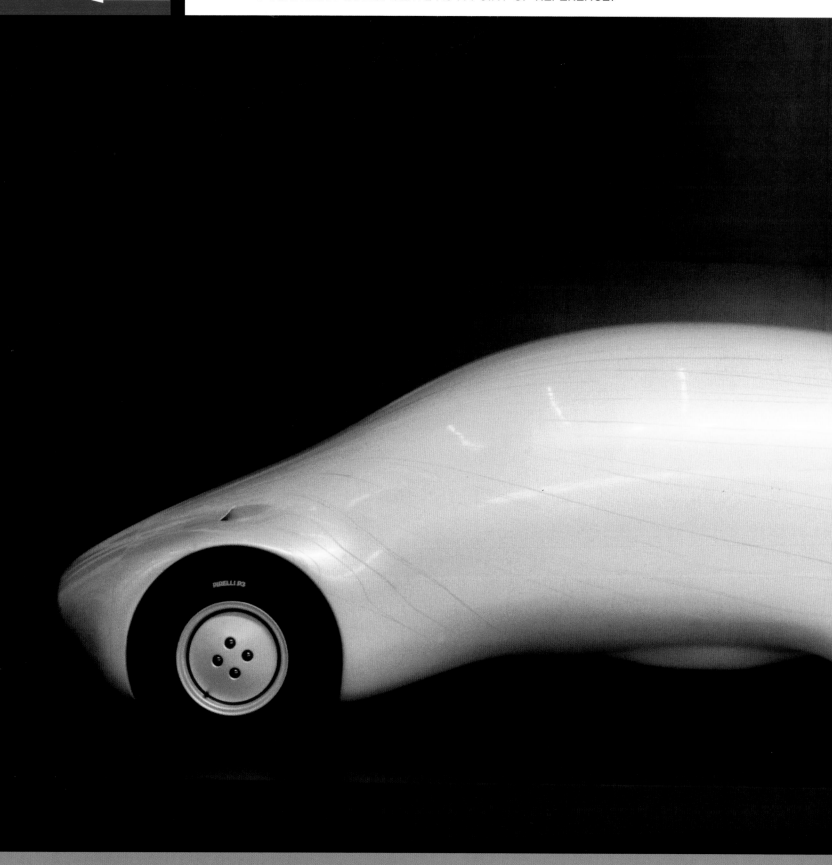

CNR-PF (PININFARINA)

Turin, **April 1978**. Aerodynamics were not something to be shirked in these difficult times. Production vehicles were systematically put through the windtunnel in order to optimise their aerodynamic performance. The point of reference in this domain became the extraordinary CNR-PF created by Pininfarina in response to a commission from Italy's National Research Council (CNR).

The CNR-PF was an idealised shape destined to become etched in the mind during the most alarmist period of the energy crisis. The original mock-up claimed a Cd of 0.172 while retaining a passenger compartment of acceptable size for four people. The lines had been evolved with real-world mechanicals in mind, properly cooled. The envelope was as smooth as a pebble, as sensual as a Henry Moore sculpture. The total absence of the slightest opening, of the slightest accessory, or of even any glazing, naturally helped it be seen as an idealised conception of reality. Thanks to the extended rear overhang, the CNR-PF took up more room than the Fiat Ritmo (Strada) that had served as a benchmark, ending up 432cm long, 167.5cm wide and 133.5 high, this on a 255.5cm wheelbase.

For Pininfarina, needless to say, it wasn't a question of stopping things there, but rather to prove that the study could move beyond being merely a statement of intent. Having come up with the perfect shape, the stylists set about making it viable, transforming it into a prototype that could be built, with doors, windows, lighting, door mirrors and all the other equipment necessary for a road car.

With aerodynamicism becoming an essential energy-saving science, Pininfarina came up with an extreme proposal, arrived at in association with Italy's National Research Council.

JAGUAR XJ-SPIDER (PININFARINA)

FORD LUCANO (GHIA)

JAGUAR XJ-SPIDER (PININFARINA) **Birmingham, October 1978**. Cabriolet based on the XJ-S, and which with its soft lines was very much in the mould of the E-type. Engine: 5,343cc V12. Power: 289bhp at 5,500rpm. Length: 460cm. Width: 183cm. Height: 118cm. Wheelbase: 259cm. Maximum speed: 150mph.

LANCIA SIBILO (BERTONE)

LANCIA SIBILO (BERTONE) **Turin, April 1978**. Mid-engined two-seater coupé built on a Lancia Stratos HF platform lengthened by 20cm. The glazing melded visually with the bodywork, giving the impression of a one-piece sculpture; Marcello Gandini was the stylist responsible. Engine: 2.4-litre V6. Length: 382.3cm. Width: 189.6cm. Height: 103cm. Wheelbase: 228cm.

LANCIA MEGAGAMMA (ITAL DESIGN)

LANCIA MEGAGAMMA (ITAL DESIGN)
Turin, April 1978. Four-door one-box design with four conventionally-hinged doors and folding rear seats, based on the Lancia Gamma. At the same time Ital Design presented the M8, a streamlined saloon (Cd 0.24) on the same platform. Engine: 2,484cc flat-four. Power: 140bhp at 5,400rpm. Length: 431cm. Width: 178cm. Height: 161.7cm. Wheelbase: 267cm.

FORD ACTION (GHIA)
Turin, April 1978. Mock-up for an extravagantly-lined aerodynamic coupé, powered by a mid-mounted 3-litre DFV V8 Cosworth F1 engine. Length: 391.2cm. Width: 190.4cm. Height: 100.3cm. Wheelbase: 241.5cm.

FORD ACTION (GHIA)

DOME-O

ECOS (PININFARINA) **Turin, April 1978**. Project for a compact fwd electric vehicle. Power: 35bhp at 4,000rpm. Length: 340.5cm. Width: 160.5cm. Height: 148cm. Wheelbase: 220cm. Maximum speed: 56mph.

FORD LUCANO (GHIA)
Turin, April 1978. Two-seater coupé based on the Ford Escort; its compactness was said to have been inspired 'by the general reduction in car size being imposed in North America'. At the same show Ghia also displayed the Fiesta-based Microsport. Engine: 1.1-litre up to 2-litre 4-cyl. Length: 423.9cm. Width: 161cm. Height: 126cm. Wheelbase: 240.5cm.

DOME-O **Geneva, March 1978**. Mid-engined GT with an abrupt but nonetheless well-mastered style. In May 1978 this Japanese creation became the SP-2. Engine: 2.8-litre 6-cyl. Power: 145bhp. Length: 423.5cm. Width: 177.5cm. Height: 99cm. Wheelbase: 245cm. Weight: 950kg.

VAUXHALL EQUUS

VAUXHALL EQUUS
Birmingham, October 1978. Roadster based on the Vauxhall-derived Panther Lima chassis; designed by Wayne Cherry. Engine: 2.3-litre 4-cyl. Length: 421.4cm. Width: 156cm. Height: 123cm. Wheelbase: 249.7cm.

ECOS (PININFARINA)

FAIRCHILD-HILLER NY STATE SAFETY SEDAN

VOLVO TUNDRA (BERTONE)

FAIRCHILD-HILLER NY STATE SAFETY SEDAN New York, 1979. The work of Hiller's Republic Aviation division, this monstrous saloon, developed to give the very best in passive safety, only assured the protection of its occupants up to 15mph.

VOLVO TUNDRA (BERTONE) Geneva, March 1979. Four-seater coupé based on the Volvo 343, designed by Marcello Gandini. Length: 402.3cm. Width: 171cm. Height: 127.7cm. Wheelbase: 239.5cm.

SBARRO ROYALE

FORD GTK (GHIA)

SBARRO ROYALE

Geneva, March 1979. With the fad for replicas at full blast, Franco Sbarro turned to the mythical Bugatti Royale; the body was in plastic and the 90deg V16 was made up from two coupled Rover V8s, mated to an automatic gearbox. Engine: 7,064cc V16. Power: 340bhp. Length: 600cm. Width: 190cm. Height: 205cm. Wheelbase: 385cm. Wheels: 700 x 17in.

FORD GTK (GHIA)

Geneva, March 1979. Estate based on a stretched Fiesta floorpan. At the same show Ghia displayed the short-wheelbase (203.2cm) Microsport. Engine: 1,117cc 4-cyl. Length: 403.1cm. Width: 166cm. Height: 124.1cm. Wheelbase: 238.8cm..

TOYOTA CX-80 Tokyo, November 1979. Two-box compact city car, distinguished by its digital electronic instrumentation, the disposition of its headlamps, and its unusual side-window treatment. Shown at Birmingham in 1980.

FORD NAVARRE (GHIA)

FORD NAVARRE (GHIA) New York, April 1979. Five-seater coupé based on the Ford Granada/Mercury Monarch. Engine: 5-litre V8. Length: 482cm. Wheelbase: 279cm.

FORD PROBE I

FORD PROBE I

Frankfurt, September 1979. Aerodynamic (Cd 0.25) coupé, first in a line of Probes; designed under Donald F Kopka. A mock-up, the car was motorised for display at Geneva in 1981.

FORD MUSTANG RSX (GHIA)

FORD MUSTANG RSX (GHIA) Frankfurt, September 1979. Two-seater coupé based on a shortened Mustang floorpan. Engine: 2.3-litre 4-cyl. Length: 419cm. Width: 170cm. Height: 127.5cm. Wheelbase: 240.8cm.

TOYOTA CX-80

THIS FUTURISTIC PROJECT, DELIBERATELY UNREALISTIC, DEMONSTRATED CITROËN'S WISH TO SET UP A TRUE STYLING STUDIO. THE KARIN SYMBOLISED THE ARRIVAL OF TREVOR FIORE AT THE HEAD OF THIS TEAM.

CITROËN KARIN

Paris, October 1980. After the death of Flaminio Bertoni, the sculptor of genius who had shaped all Citroëns since the Traction Avant, Robert Opron took his place with panache and humility, to oversee the development of such landmark vehicles as the SM, GS and CX. In 1975, after 13 years at Citroën, Opron left to run Renault's styling department. For several years Citroën's styling section had nobody really leading it, although Jean Giret unofficially fulfilled that rôle, under the obscurantist tutelage of the design office headed by Xavier Karcher.

In January 1980 Trevor Fiore was summoned to reinstate a styling studio at Citroën. A seductive and widely-travelled stylist, Sheffield-born Fiore (original name Trevor Frost) had carried out design work for TVR, Elva, Monteverdi and Daf. In 1979 he became a consultant to Citroën, and was appointed director of its *Centre du Style* on 1 July 1980. The Karin was his first act of faith. With its pyramidal shape and its futurist interior, it represented the reconstruction of the Citroën style. The Karin was an authentic 'dream vehicle', a gullwing-door coupé with three front seats and a central driving position. Unmotorised, it had relatively tightly-drawn dimensions, with a length of 370cm, a width of 190cm and a height of 107.5cm.

Also playing a key part in the Karin was Michel Harmand. At Citroën since April 1964, he had become responsible for the *Formes Intérieures* section in 1976. A graduate of the Beaux-Arts, in painting and then in decorative arts and interior architecture, Harmand always sought intelligent solutions that avoided the stultifyingly obvious. This enlightened creator came up with the *lunule* instrument panel for the CX, and the steering-column control satellites for the Visa. After a spell at Peugeot from 1987, Harmand went on to teach at Strate College, the most renowned in France for its design course.

The pyramid shape of the Karin necessitated an unusual seating arrangement, with a central driving position and two flanking seats set back on either side.

LANCIA MEDUSA (ITAL DESIGN)

LANCIA MEDUSA (ITAL DESIGN) **Turin, April 1980**.
Four-door mid-engined aerodynamic saloon (Cd 0.263)
based on a stretched Lancia Monte Carlo platform –
remarkable treatment of volumes and in particular of the
sides. Subsequently shown in Los Angeles (1980) and
Geneva (1981). Engine: 1,995cc 4-cyl. Power: 120bhp.
Length: 440.5cm. Width: 181.3cm. Height: 126.3cm.
Wheelbase: 279cm.

RENAULT EVE **Paris,
October 1980**. Research
vehicle to investigate
energy saving through
optimised aerodynamics
(Cd 0.239) and powertrain
management; based on
the Renault 18. Running in
June 1981, Eve evolved
into Eve+ in October 1983.
Engine: 1,108cc 4-cyl.
Power: 39bhp at
5,500rpm. Transmission:
automatic. Length:
440.8cm. Width: 174cm.
Wheelbase: 250.9cm.
Weight: 845kg. Maximum
speed: 98mph.

RENAULT EVE

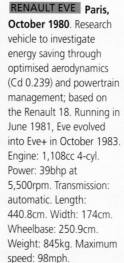

FORD PROBE II

FORD PROBE II
Geneva, March 1980.
Second in the Probe series,
this five-door two-box
saloon (Cd 0.30) was more
of a realistic proposition
than the Probe I. It
signalled the arrival in
1980 of Donald F Kopka as
chief of the Ford Design
Centre. Engine: 4-cyl petrol
or diesel. Length: 454.9cm.
Width: 178.8cm. Height:
133.3cm. Wheelbase:
255cm.

FORD ALTAIR (GHIA)

LAMBORGHINI ATHON (BERTONE)

LAMBORGHINI ATHON (BERTONE) **Turin, April 1980**. Two-seater roadster with
transverse mid engine, designed by Marc Deschamps; his first creation for Bertone, to
which he had come from Renault the previous year. Engine: 2,996cc V8. Power: 260bhp
at 7,500rpm. Length: 397cm. Width: 188.8cm. Height: 107cm. Wheelbase: 245.5cm.
Maximum speed: 150mph.

ASTON MARTIN BULLDOG **Los Angeles, May
1980**. Mid-engined GT in the angular style so typical of
William Towns, already responsible for the 1978 Aston
Martin Lagonda. Engine: 5,340cc V8 twin-turbo. Gearbox:
ZF 5-sp. Length: 472.4cm. Width: 156.4cm. Height:
109.2cm. Wheelbase: 276.9cm. Maximum speed:
190mph.

FORD ALTAIR (GHIA)
Geneva, March 1980.
Four-door saloon based on
a Granada floorpan
lengthened by 5.1cm.
Angular but aerodynamic
(Cd 0.35) wedge-shaped
three-box body designed
by Paul Breuer. Engine:
2.8-litre V6. Length:
468.6cm. Width: 189.2cm.
Height: 134.4cm.
Wheelbase: 277cm.

ASTON MARTIN BULLDOG

FORD MONTANA LOBO (GHIA)

FERRARI PININ (PININFARINA)

FERRARI PININ (PININFARINA) **Turin, April 1980**.
Four-door front-engined saloon, designed by Diego
Ottina, under Leonardo Fioravanti, for Pininfarina's
50th birthday. The prototype was intensively tested
before the project was ultimately abandoned. Engine:
4,943cc flat-12. Power: 360bhp. Length: 483cm. Width:
182cm. Height: 131cm. Wheelbase: 275cm.

FORD MONTANA LOBO (GHIA) **New York, April
1980**. One of the first attempts in a concept car to exploit
the diversification in the use of 4x4s. Polyvalent, it was
intended as much for leisure as for rougher work. Also
displayed in 1980, at Detroit, was the Mercury Antser.
Engine: 5-litre V8. Length: 479.8cm. Width: 191.5cm.
Height: 196.6cm. Wheelbase: 272.5cm.

FIAT VSS (IDEA)

LOLA SPÉCIALE (MICHELOTTI)

LOLA SPÉCIALE (MICHELOTTI) Geneva, March
1981. Two-seat mid-engined GT based on a Chevrolet-powered Lola chassis. Engine: 8.2-litre V8. Power: 620bhp. Length: 408cm. Width: 177cm. Height: 107cm. Wheelbase: 246cm. Weight: 1,350kg.

AC (GHIA) Geneva,
March 1981. Coupé based on the mid-engined AC ME3000: relative to the standard car, Ghia's offering was much more graceful. Other Ghia concept cars for 1981 were the Super Gnat (Detroit), the Avant-garde (Geneva), and the Cockpit (Geneva). Engine: 2,994cc V6. Power: 138bhp at 5,000rpm. Length: 389cm. Width: 151cm. Height: 117cm. Wheelbase: 117cm.

AC (GHIA)

FORD PROBE III

Frankfurt, September 1981. Five-door saloon (Cd 0.22) anticipating the Ford Sierra, created under Uwe Bahnsen, 1976–86 head of design for Ford of Europe. It was developed as part of a programme encouraged by West Germany's Ministry of Research and Technology. Other concept cars at Frankfurt included the Audi Forschungsauto, the Karmann Uni-Car, the Mercedes-Benz Forschungs-PKW, the Opel Tech 1, and the Volkswagen Auto 2000. Engine: 1,593cc 4-cyl. Power: 68bhp. Length: 463.6cm. Width: 174cm. Height: 132.1cm. Wheelbase: 258.9cm. Maximum speed: 109mph.

FORD PROBE III

GENERAL MOTORS AERO X-CAR Detroit, June
1981. Streamlined saloon (Cd 0.285) that kicked off a series of GM studies on aerodynamic efficiency, under the authority of Irvin Rybicki, head of GM design staff from 1977 until 1986; based on the Chevrolet Cavalier platform. Engine: 2,471cc 4-cyl. Power: 85bhp at 4,000rpm. Wheelbase: 266.5cm.

GENERAL MOTORS AERO X-CAR

MAZDA MX-81 (BERTONE) Tokyo, November
1981. Four-seater coupé based on the 323 Turbo and designed under the direction of Marc Deschamps; latterly shown at Turin in 1982. The interior was by Eugenio Pagliano and featured the steering wheel being replaced by a belt that ran around a screen giving all the information needed by the driver. Engine: 1,490cc 4-cyl. Power: 130bhp at 6,000rpm. Length: 394cm. Width: 169cm. Height: 128cm. Wheelbase: 263.5cm.

FIAT VSS (IDEA) Turin,
October 1981. Modular vehicle (*Vettura Sperimentale a Sottosistemi*) characterised by its spaceframe base-unit structure which could accept different subsidiary elements depending on the type of body chosen. The VSS was conceived by the architect Renzo Piano, co-founder of the I.DE.A institute and a board member from 1978 until 1981. Engine: 1.1-litre to 2-litre 4-cyl. Wheelbase: 245cm.

CITROËN XÉNIA

Frankfurt, September 1981. One-box saloon styled under Trevor Fiore, with an original treatment of the rear side windows and C-post. The mock-up is preserved at the Musée Nationale de l'Automobile in Mulhouse. Engine: 1,299cc flat-four. Power: 65bhp at 5,500rpm. Length: 420cm. Width: 175cm. Height: 123cm. Wheelbase: 255cm.

AUDI QUARTZ (PININFARINA)

AUDI QUARTZ (PININFARINA) Geneva, March
1981. Coupé based on the 4wd Audi Quattro, and dedicated to the Swiss *Revue Automobile* on its 75th birthday. The elliptical-lensed headlights were produced by Carello. Engine: 2,144cc turbo 5-cyl. Power: 200bhp at 5,500rpm. Length: 413.5cm. Width: 176.5cm. Height: 126.5cm. Wheelbase: 252.5cm. Weight: 1,315kg.

CITROËN XÉNIA

MAZDA MX-81 (BERTONE)

By means of the Capsula Giorgio Giugiaro yet again demonstrated his talent for imagining new concepts for cars of the future, notably in optimising the relationship between accommodation and external size.

Turin, April 1982. Under the banner of Ital Design, which he established in 1968, Giorgio Giugiaro made his mark as a formidable pioneer in the creation of ground-breaking solutions to the challenges presented by the motor-car. After the New York Taxi of 1976 and the Megagamma of 1978, Giugiaro tackled the question of the one-box 'monospace' from another angle. The Capsula was conceived a little in the fashion of touring coaches, with a lower deck enclosing the space for luggage, tools and spare parts. The passenger cabin was thus built on a markedly raised floor. As it turned out, the resultant interior space on the prototype had a generous glass area and was very comfortable. The floor was completely unobstructed around the individual front seats and in front of the rear bench seat; access was via wide gullwing doors. Beyond the prototype's MPV-saloon bodywork all sorts of coachwork could be envisaged on the same platform. Countless more utilitarian variations were suggested, from an ambulance to a breakdown truck, from a mini-bus to a delivery van, from a fire engine to a pick-up, and so on.

The Capsula was based on the mechanicals of the Alfasud (a 1,490cc flat-four developing 105bhp at 6,000rpm). The car's size was remarkably modest, with it measuring only 372cm long, for a width of 177cm and a height of 166cm, this on a 240cm wheelbase; weight was 950kg.

At the same show Ital Design unveiled the Orca, a completely different and much more conventional proposition. Giorgio Giugiaro thus expressed his conviction that the car of the future would evolve while diversifying, and that new formats for the family car would develop in parallel with the traditional saloon.

ALFA ROMEO CAPSULA (ITAL DESIGN)

The idea of the MPV was in the air, but it was necessary to wait until 1982 to see the arrival of the Nissan Prairie, until 1983 for the Chrysler Voyager, and 1984 for the Renault Espace.

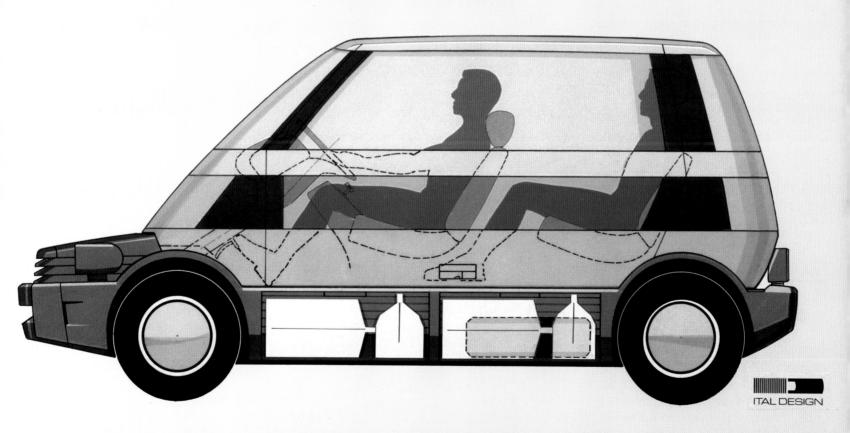

RENAULT VESTA

FORD BREZZA (GHIA)

Turin, April 1982. Two-seater coupé based on the Ford EXP, with an aerodynamic (Cd 0.30 approx) body designed by a female stylist, Marinela Corvasce. Engine: 1.6-litre 4-cyl CVH. Transmission: automatic. Length: 399.6cm. Width: 164cm. Height: 122.8cm. Wheelbase: 231.6cm.

FORD BREZZA (GHIA)

LUCAS HYBRID ELECTRIC CAR (OGLE)

RUK 986Y

LUCAS HYBRID ELECTRIC CAR (OGLE) **Birmingham, October 1982**. Five-door saloon built by Reliant in conjunction with Lucas Chloride EV Systems Ltd; plastic body with steel doors. Hybrid power, with a Reliant 848cc four-cylinder engine at the front, linked to a 50kW Lucas electric motor. Length: 436.7cm. Width: 173cm. Height: 158cm. Wheelbase: 254cm. Weight: 2,240kg. Maximum speed: 85mph.

RENAULT VESTA **Paris, October 1982**. Fuel-consumption research vehicle (Cd 0.25), achieving less than 3litres/100km (94.2mpg). The first of the six Vesta prototypes ran at Montlhéry in October 1983 – and the Vesta 2 managed 2.8 litres/100km in 1987. Engine: 716cc 3-cyl. Transmission: 5-speed. Length: 327cm. Wheelbase: 225cm. Weight: 510kg.

SAAB VIKING (RAYTON FISSORE)

GENERAL MOTORS AERO 2000

GENERAL MOTORS AERO 2000 **Orlando, October 1982**. Four-seater coupé (Cd 0.23) shown at the Epcot Center 'World of Motion'. Further GM aerodynamic studies were the Aero 2002 (1982; Cd 0.14), the Chevrolet Citation IV (1983; Cd 0.18), the Express (1987; Cd 0.195), and the Aero 2003A (1987; Cd 0.166). Engine: 3-cyl turbo-diesel. Power: 68bhp. Length: 435.6cm. Width: 165.1cm. Height: 118.1cm. Wheelbase: 260.9cm. Weight: 817kg.

SAAB VIKING (RAYTON FISSORE) **Turin, April 1982**. Four-seater coupé based on the Saab 900 and shown in Turin and then in Los Angeles in the spring of 1982; styled by Tom Tjaarda for coachbuilder Rayton Fissore. Other concept cars at Turin included Open Design's Starwind and Ipothesis. Engine: 1,985cc 4-cyl. Power: 100bhp. Length: 448cm. Width: 167cm. Height: 137cm. Wheelbase: 251.5cm.

SBARRO SUPER TWELVE

FORD QUICK SILVER (GHIA) **Geneva, March 1982**. This time Ghia tried a mid-engine installation in a five-seater saloon; the car (Cd 0.30) was based on the 1981 AC study, and was the work of Delio Meinardi. Engine: 3-litre V6. Transmission: 5-speed. Length: 456cm. Width: 175cm. Height: 126.5cm. Wheelbase: 259cm.

LANCIA ORCA (ITAL DESIGN)

SBARRO SUPER TWELVE **Geneva, March 1982**. Compact sporting 2+2 saloon with 12-cylinder in-line mid-mounted engine made of two 6-cyl 1,286cc Kawazaki Z-1300A engines joined together. A similar recipe produced the Super Eight (Geneva 1984). Power: 250bhp. Length: 315cm. Width: 175cm. Height: 130cm. Wheelbase: 220cm. Weight: 750kg.

FORD QUICK SILVER (GHIA)

LANCIA ORCA (ITAL DESIGN) **Turin, April 1982**. Four-door saloon based on the Lancia Delta Turbo 4x4; it continued the quest for optimised aerodynamics (Cd 0.245) whilst retaining modest dimensions and sensible lines. Engine: 1,585cc 4-cyl. Power: 140bhp. Length: 438.8cm. Width: 172.8cm. Height: 137.5cm. Wheelbase: 267.5cm.

RENAULT GABBIANO (ITAL DESIGN)

RENAULT GABBIANO (ITAL DESIGN) **Geneva, March 1983**. Four-seater coupé based on the Renault 11; the long gullwing doors gave shared access to the front and rear seats. Engine: 1,397cc 4-cyl. Power: 72bhp at 5,750rpm. Length: 390cm. Width: 164cm. Height: 128.5cm. Wheelbase: 248cm.

TOYOTA FX-1

TOYOTA FX-1 **Tokyo, November 1983**. Front-engined 2+2 coupé (Cd 0.25) built on backbone chassis; hydropneumatic suspension allowing speed-sensitive electronic adjustment of ground clearance. Engine: 2-litre 6-cyl dohc 24v. Power: 250bhp.

VOLVO LCP 2000

Göteborg, June 1983. Front-wheel-drive two-box prototype (Cd 0.25) exploring weight-saving ('Light Component Project'), built with intensive use of magnesium. The back seats were rearward-facing, and the tailgate opening extended into the roof, borrowing from a 1960s Studebaker idea. Designed by Jan Wilsgaard but built by IAD. Engine: 1,279cc 3-cyl turbo-diesel. Power: 52bhp at 4,300rpm. Length: 398cm. Width: 165cm. Height: 130cm. Wheelbase: 254cm. Weight: 645kg. Fuel consumption: 78.5mpg. Maximum speed: 112mph.

VOLVO LCP 2000

ALFA ROMEO ZETA 6 (ZAGATO)

ALFA ROMEO ZETA 6 (ZAGATO) **Geneva, March 1983**. Sensual-lined coupé based on the Alfa Romeo GTV6 and designed by Giuseppe Mittino under Miro Galuzzi, chief of Zagato Industrial Design. Despite some effects borrowed from the Porsche 928, the Zeta was very much in the Zagato tradition. Engine: 2,492cc V6. Power: 160bhp at 5,800rpm.

OPEL JUNIOR **Frankfurt, September 1983**. Minimalist vehicle (Cd 0.31) for young people, designed by H Kodama under Wayne Cherry (successor in 1983 to Gordon Brown) and George Gallion. The dashboard was designed to take removable plug-in square accessory modules (clock, rev-counter, etc). Built on a shortened Corsa/Nova platform. Engine: 1.2-litre 4-cyl. Power: 55bhp. Length: 341cm. Width: 157cm. Height: 145cm.

OPEL JUNIOR

VOLANIS HÉLIOS

Geneva, March 1983. One-box compact saloon (Cd 0.22) with four separate seats; not a runner. Created by Antoine Volanis, who had gone independent in 1980 after having worked for Matra. Length: 394cm. Width: 168cm. Height: 150cm.

VOLANIS HÉLIOS

ALFA ROMEO DELFINO (BERTONE) **Geneva, March 1983**. Coupé based on the Alfa 6, designed by Marc Deschamps. His style was characterised by clearly structured volumes, broken up by complex shutlines, resulting in softer contours than on the cars of his predecessor Marcello Gandini. Engine: 2,492cc V6. Power: 160bhp at 5,800rpm. Length: 414cm. Width: 183cm. Height: 118cm. Wheelbase: 260cm.

ALFA ROMEO DELFINO (BERTONE)

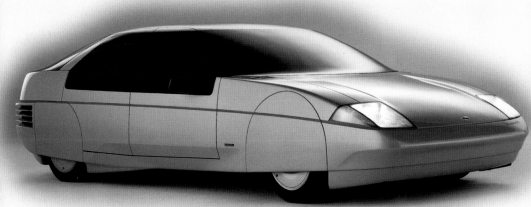

FORD PROBE IV

FORD PROBE IV **Detroit, January 1983**. Aerodynamic hatchback with a record 0.15 Cd while remaining a practical saloon; steel and Kevlar body by Ghia. Faired-in wheels and adjustable ground clearance. Engine: 1.6-litre 4-cyl. Power: 102bhp at 4,500rpm. Length: 475.5cm. Width: 182.6cm. Height: 120.2cm. Wheelbase: 271.8cm. Tyres: P155/75 R16.

IN THE MIDST OF THE 1980S, HOPE RETURNED. EVEN THE WORTHY FIRM OF PEUGEOT TOOK TO DREAMING, PONDERING ON THE FUTURE AS A WAY OF GIVING A RESONANCE TO ITS SPORTING SUCCESSES THROUGH THE CONSTRUCTION OF DREAM CARS OF ITS OWN.

Paris, October 1984. One day in the summer of 1984, the duo of Gérard Welter (for the exterior) and Paul Bracq (for the interior) decided to put to one side their daily constraints. These two figures from the car styling world represented opposite poles. Gérard Welter had succeeded Paul Bouvot, who had run Peugeot's styling department, and had the difficult task of managing the design competition between Peugeot and Pininfarina. This discreet and sombre creator had a passion for motor-racing, a passion which he assuaged through the production of the WM sports-racers. Paul Bracq, on the other hand, was a flamboyant artist, brought up at Mercedes-Benz and BMW, before crossing over to orchestrate interior styling at Peugeot.

The contrast of colours in the passenger compartment was an echo of the violence of the exterior forms: blue carpet, red leather, electric and aggressive tonalities. Anchored to the centre console, the instrument binnacle seemed to be

PEUGEOT QUASAR

suspended in space. The electronics twinkled with all their liquid crystals, sparkling on a screen to send out signals of a naked futurism; this side of the car had been developed by Clarion.

The mechanicals were derived from the 205 Turbo 16, twice winner of the World Rally Championship, in 1985 and 1986. Thus the

running gear used double-wishbone suspension with levers and bell-cranks to reduce unsprung weight, as well as the T16's ventilated disc brakes. The engine was the twin-cam four-cylinder twin-turbo unit, delivering 600bhp and 367lb ft of torque; it was mated to a five-speed gearbox.

Peugeot hadn't got us used to such enthusiastic diversions. The Quasar was the work of Gérard Welter for the exterior and Paul Bracq for the interior; the painting on the left is also by Bracq.

CITROËN ECO 2000

HONDA STUDIO HPX (PININFARINA)

HONDA STUDIO HPX (PININFARINA) Turin, **November 1984**. Study built around an F2 Honda RA264E engine in tribute to the fruitful collaboration between the styling house and Honda. The aerodynamic body was 'ground effect', but it was only a mock-up…. The car was created under Leonardo Fioravanti, head of Pininfarina *Studi e Ricerche* from February 1982 until December 1987. Engine: 1,996cc V6. Length: 416.5cm. Width: 177cm. Height: 112.5cm. Wheelbase: 255cm.

CITROËN ECO 2000 **Paris, October 1984**. The objective of the ECO 2000 programme was to lower fuel consumption to 3 litres per 100km (94.2mpg). Three prototypes – SA 103, SA 117 and SA 109 – were built between 1982 and 1984 under the umbrella of PSA's Advanced Styling studio at Carrières-sous-Poissy directed by Arthur (Art) Blakeslee. Engine: 749cc 3-cyl. Power: 35bhp. Cd: 0.21. Length: 349cm. Weight: 480kg.

VOLANIS APOLLON

VOLANIS APOLLON
Paris, October 1984.
Aerodynamic saloon (Cd 0.13) based on the Renault 11 Turbo and designed by Antoine Volanis. Length: 455cm.

FIAT GOBI (MAGGIORA)
Turin, November 1984.
Rustic vehicle based on the Fiat Panda 4x4; designed by Paolo Martin and built by Maggiora. Engine: 965cc 4-cyl. Power: 48bhp. Length: 336cm. Width: 154cm. Height: 135.5cm. Wheelbase: 216cm.

LOTUS ETNA (ITAL DESIGN)

LOTUS ETNA (ITAL DESIGN) **Birmingham, October 1984**. Prototype for a mid-engined GT ordered by Lotus and based on the Esprit. It was fitted with the new Type 909 Lotus V8 power unit. Engine: 4-litre V8. Power: 350bhp at 6,500rpm. Length: 426.8cm. Width: 184.4cm. Height: 114.3cm. Wheelbase: 251.5cm.

CHEVROLET RAMARRO (BERTONE)

CHEVROLET RAMARRO (BERTONE) **Los Angeles, May 1984**. Coupé based on the Chevrolet Corvette, created for the Olympic Games in Los Angeles; subsequently shown at the 1984 Paris salon and rewarded with the *Auto & Design* Car Design Award. Engine: 5.7-litre V8. Power: 205bhp. Length: 415cm. Width: 192cm. Height: 119cm. Wheelbase: 245cm. Weight: 1,400kg.

FIAT GOBI (MAGGIORA)

LANCIA TOGETHER (ITAL DESIGN)

LANCIA TOGETHER (ITAL DESIGN) **Turin, November 1984**. Monospace based on the Lancia Delta HF, shown alongside the Marlin, a conventional saloon on the same platform. Engine: 1,585cc 4-cyl. Power: 130bhp at 5,600rpm. Length: 415cm. Width: 179cm. Height: 160cm. Wheelbase: 268cm.

VOLKSWAGEN STUDENT

VOLKSWAGEN STUDENT **Geneva, March 1984**. Economic urban 2+2 (Cd 0.30) in which the number of elements comprising the body were kept to the absolute minimum. Engine: 1,100cc 4-cyl. Power: 50/75bhp. Length: 313cm. Width: 151cm. Height: 132cm. Maximum speed: 98–110mph.

MITSUBISHI MP90X

MG EX-E

MITSUBISHI MP90X **Tokyo, November 1985**. Futuristic coupé (Cd 0.22) distinguished by its all-enclosing sides and its tail dominated by a 'carrying handle' spoiler. Computer electronics featured extensively in the instrumentation and navigation systems. Four-wheel steering and composite-construction bodyshell.

MG EX-E **Frankfurt, September 1985**. Practical proposition for a targa-top mid-engined coupé (Cd 0.24), based on the MG Metro 6R4. The design director was Roy Axe, who had arrived at Austin-Rover in 1982. Aluminium chassis and plastic body. Engine: 3-litre dohc 24v V6. Power: 253bhp at 7,000rpm. Maximum speed: 170mph.

NISSAN CUE-X

NISSAN CUE-X **Tokyo, November 1985**. Classic *grande routière* saloon (Cd 0.24), with 4wd and four-wheel steering. Engine: 3-litre Plasma-VG-X 6-cyl. Power: 300bhp. Length: 486cm. Width: 185cm. Height: 130.5cm. Wheelbase: 280cm.

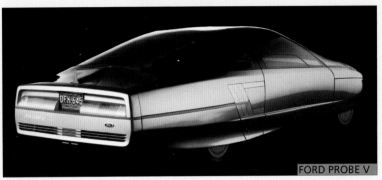

FORD PROBE V

FORD PROBE V **Frankfurt, September 1985**. Aerodynamic 2+2 coupé (transverse mid-engine) with a record 0.137 coefficient of drag. Latterly exhibited in Paris in April 1989. Engine: 1.9-litre 16v turbo 4-cyl. Power: 185bhp at 4,800rpm. Length: 486.6cm. Width: 175.5cm. Height: 119.4cm. Wheelbase: 274.3cm.

MAZDA MX-03

MAZDA MX-03 **Frankfurt, September 1985**. Four-seater coupé (Cd 0.25) following up on the MX-02 saloon shown at Tokyo in 1983. Aircraft-cockpit dashboard, 4wd, four-wheel steering. Engine: 654cc triple-rotor Wankel. Power: 320bhp at 7,000rpm. Length: 451cm. Width: 180cm. Height: 120cm.

BUICK WILDCAT

BUICK WILDCAT **Las Vegas, November 1985**. Shown at the SEMA, this coupé by Buick Special Products was given the *Car Design* Award. The body, developed by PPG Industries from a design by David P Rand, featured a cockpit cover pivoting in its entirety to the front. Engine: 3,791cc 24v V6. Power: 230bhp at 6,000rpm. Transmission: 4-speed automatic. Length: 438.8cm. Width: 183.6cm. Height: 111cm. Wheelbase: 259.1cm. Weight: 1,320kg.

SBARRO CHALLENGE **Geneva, March 1985**. Mid-engined 4wd coupé (Cd 0.25) designed by Camille Diebold under the direction of Franco Sbarro. Engine: 5-litre turbo V8 (Mercedes-Benz). Power: 380bhp. Length: 422cm. Width: 198cm. Height: 100cm. Wheelbase: 272cm. Weight: 1,400kg.

SAAB EV-1

SBARRO CHALLENGE

SAAB EV-1 **Los Angeles, May 1985**. Four-seater coupé (Cd 0.32) based on the Saab 900 Turbo 16. Air-conditioning powered by solar cells in the roof. Styled under the direction of Björn Envall, in charge of Saab design since 1969. Length: 430cm. Weight: 1,150kg.

WITH CREATIONS OF THIS DEPTH OF QUALITY, GENERAL MOTORS LENT ITS IMPRIMATUR TO THE BIO-DESIGN SCHOOL OF STYLING. THE INDY SUGGESTED YET AGAIN THAT ONE DAY THERE MIGHT BE A MID-ENGINED CORVETTE.

Chicago, February 1986. The place is mythical. Go into the GM Design building, and it is as if nothing has changed since the departure of Harley J Earl in 1958. It's still the same office, with its pale oak inlays to a design by Earl himself, still the same furniture with its 'modern' geometric effects that are so 1950s, still the same bay-windows, opening on one side onto that rectangular lake with its futuristic fountain and on the other onto the Auditorium, a sci-fi cupola. We're at the heart of the GM Technical Center, a town within the town of Warren, one of the districts that makes up the megapolis of Detroit. Nothing has changed of that functional décor thought up by the Finnish engineer Eero Saarinen in 1956. It's still at the Tech Center that the future of America is brewed up.

In the middle of the 1980s the car industry was recovering from the energy crisis. Head of GM Design Staff from 1977 to 1986, Irvin Rybicki had the thankless task of living through the

CHEVROLET CORVETTE INDY

Among the numerous prototypes evoking the possible creation of a mid-engined Corvette, the Corvette Indy was one of the most successful and plausible.

calling into question of the US automotive industry. An austere and discreet man, he was not such a media darling as his predecessors Harley Earl and Bill Mitchell, but it was under his direction that the American motor-car underwent one of its most significant revolutions.

The Corvette Indy, a mid-engined GT, had a strong technological content. Its lines explored with success the potential of organic forms while playing with the subtlety of bio-design in the exterior volumes as much as in the interior fittings. The engine, a 600bhp quad-cam 32-valve V8 of 2,650cc, was derived from a power unit designed for Indy and CART single-seaters, while the running gear, and most notably the suspension, was developed with Lotus. This included 4wd, four-wheel steering, traction control, and anti-lock brakes. The car was subsequently shown at SEMA (Specialty Equipment Market Association) in Las Vegas and it underwent intensive dynamic testing. Originally in silver-grey, it was later painted red.

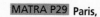
VOLKSWAGEN SCOOTER

VOLKSWAGEN SCOOTER **Geneva, March 1986**. Three-wheeled fun car, created under Herbert Schäffer, head of VW-Design from 1972. Transverse front engine; Cd 0.25. Engine: 1.043cc/1400cc 4-cyl. Power: 40bhp/90bhp. Length: 318cm. Width: 150cm. Height: 123.5cm. Wheelbase: 215cm. Weight: 550kg.

CITROËN ZABRUS (BERTONE)

CITROËN ZABRUS (BERTONE) **Turin, November 1986**. Four-seater coupé (named after a beetle) based on the Citroën BX 4TC. A magnificent sculpture, playing on the car's structural volumes, and the work of Marc Deschamps (exterior) and Eugenio Pagliano (interior). Engine: 2,141cc turbo 4-cyl. Power: 200bhp. Length: 430cm. Weight: 1,080kg. Maximum speed: 137mph.

OLDSMOBILE AEROTECH

OLDSMOBILE AEROTECH **Detroit, September 1986**. GT intended for record-breaking. Styled by David North, Oldsmobile chief designer, on a March Indy chassis. In August 1987 a stretched version, the Aerotech ST, hit 267mph at Fort Stockton, Texas, in the hands of AJ Foyt. Engine: 2.3-litre 16v 'Quad 4' or 1,993cc turbo 4-cyl. Power: 850–1000bhp. Length: 488cm. Width: 218cm. Height: 102cm. Wheelbase: 283cm. Weight: 726kg.

MATRA P29 **Paris, October 1986**. Free-thinking sporting coupé concept, with numerous panels in composites; transverse mid-mounted engine. Designed by Aimé Saugues under Philippe Guédon. Engine: 1,995cc 16v 4-cyl. Power: 255bhp. Length: 410cm. Width: 183cm. Height: 130cm. Weight: 840kg.

IAD ALIEN **Turin, November 1986**. Futuristic transverse-mid-engined concept, designed by Martin Longmore and Marcus Hotback and making play on the separation between the rear drivetrain and the passenger compartment.

PONTIAC TRANS SPORT **Chicago, February 1986**. One-box design that anticipated a range of series-production models. That said, Terry Henline's design was much more harmonious than when translated to the production Trans Sport. Height: 151cm. Wheelbase: 295cm.

PEUGEOT PROXIMA **Paris, October 1986**. Futuristic coupé with a body in stratified Kevlar, incorporating solar cells on the boot-lid to power the ventilation; design directed by Gérard Welter (exterior) and Paul Bracq (interior). The gearbox and the clutch were electronically controlled. Engine: 2,850cc twin-turbo V6. Power: 600bhp at 8,000rpm. Torque: 449lb ft at 6,000rpm. Length: 442cm. Width: 206cm. Height: 114cm. Weight: 1,080kg.

MATRA P29

IAD ALIEN

PONTIAC TRANS SPORT

PEUGEOT PROXIMA

OLDSMOBILE INCAS (ITAL DESIGN)

OLDSMOBILE INCAS (ITAL DESIGN) **Turin, November 1986**. Aerodynamic four-door saloon with Oldsmobile Quad 4 engine and platform based on that of the Maya prototype. Shown at the same time as the Machimoto and the Orbit. Engine: 2,260cc turbo 4-cyl. Power: 230bhp. Length: 445cm. Width: 185cm. Height: 125cm. Wheelbase: 287.5cm.

NISSAN ARC-X

ISUZU COA-III

NISSAN ARC-X Tokyo, November 1987. Very elegant four-door saloon that won the *Car Design* award for 1987. 'Intelligent' control systems, 4wd, four-wheel steering. Other Nissan concept cars at the Tokyo show were the Saurus, Judo, Jura and Mid4/II. Engine: VG30DE dohc 24v V6. Length: 477cm. Wheelbase: 285cm.

ISUZU COA-III Tokyo, November 1987. Sporty cross-country vehicle making play of 'the coexistence of nature and civilisation'. Designed under Shiro Nakamura. Pneumatic suspension, 4wd, 4ws. Mid-mounted ceramic 1,588cc engine: 4-cyl turbo 16v, developing 170bhp.

TOYOTA GTV Tokyo, November 1987. Gas-turbine 2+2 coupé, shown alongside Toyota FXV-II concept car. Power: 150bhp at 5,300rpm. Transmission: 4-sp automatic. Length: 472.5cm. Width: 179cm. Height: 132.5cm. Wheelbase: 259.5cm. Maximum speed: 120mph.

TOYOTA GTV

SUZUKI RT-1 Tokyo, November 1987. Interesting proposal for a compact sporting 4x4 ('Runabout Sports Car'). Engine: 1.6-litre dohc 16v 4-cyl. Length: 370cm. Width: 169.5cm. Height: 152cm. Wheelbase: 235cm.

SUZUKI RT-1

ZENDER VISION 3 Frankfurt, September 1987. GT (Cd 0.342) with mid-mounted Mercedes-Benz engine, evolved from Vision 2 (Frankfurt 1985); designed by Günther Zillner. Shown as a mock-up at Essen in 1986 and extrapolated into an open version, the Vision 3C (Geneva 1986). Engine: 5.6-litre V8. Power: 300bhp. Length: 407cm. Width: 198cm. Height: 111cm. Wheelbase: 250cm. Weight: 1,350kg.

MITSUBISHI HSR

MITSUBISHI HSR Tokyo, November 1987. Mid-engined (High-Speed Research) GT, based on the mechanicals of the Galant; 5-sp gearbox, 4wd, 4ws. Evolved into the HSR-II for Tokyo 1989. Engine: 1,997cc turbo 16v 4-cyl. Power: 295bhp at 8,000rpm. Length: 460cm. Width: 181cm. Height: 118.5cm. Maximum speed: 180mph.

LAMBORGHINI PORTOFINO Frankfurt, September 1987. Saloon (Cd 0.342) with its four doors opening like wing sheaths; Jalpa engine. Built – by Coggiola – to mark Lamborghini's purchase by Chrysler. Engine: 3,485cc V8. Power: 225bhp at 7,000rpm. Length: 481cm. Width: 184cm. Height: 130cm. Wheelbase: 309cm. Weight: 1,350kg.

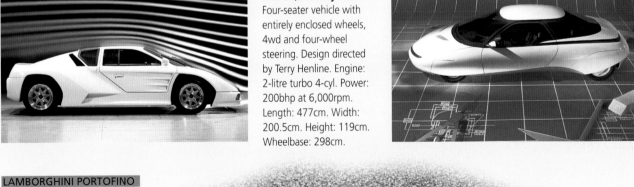

ZENDER VISION 3

PONTIAC PURSUIT Detroit, January 1987. Four-seater vehicle with entirely enclosed wheels, 4wd and four-wheel steering. Design directed by Terry Henline. Engine: 2-litre turbo 4-cyl. Power: 200bhp at 6,000rpm. Length: 477cm. Width: 200.5cm. Height: 119cm. Wheelbase: 298cm.

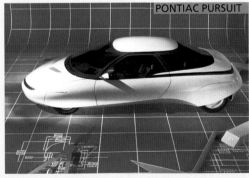

PONTIAC PURSUIT

LAMBORGHINI PORTOFINO

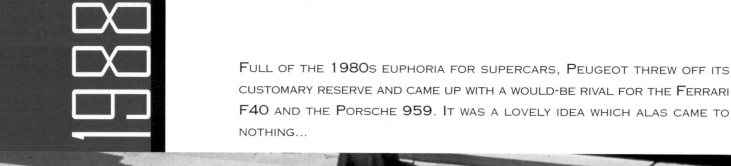
FULL OF THE 1980S EUPHORIA FOR SUPERCARS, PEUGEOT THREW OFF ITS CUSTOMARY RESERVE AND CAME UP WITH A WOULD-BE RIVAL FOR THE FERRARI F40 AND THE PORSCHE 959. IT WAS A LOVELY IDEA WHICH ALAS CAME TO NOTHING…

Paris, October 1988. Thanks to sporting director Jean Todt and technical director André de Cortanze, Peugeot had brought home a formidable number of racing honours. The 205 Turbo 16 had won the World Rally Championship in 1985 and 1986. The same car, converted for rally-raids, had won the Paris-Dakar in 1987 and 1988…

Peugeot's styling department wanted to shout about this reputation by creating a grand-touring motor-car, a concept car that would be less of a flight of fancy than the Quasar and the Proxima.

The Oxia was a coupé with a length of 461cm,

a width of 202cm (more than a Ferrari Testarossa!), and a height of 113cm, sitting on a 280cm wheelbase. It was shod with 235/45 x 17in tyres at the front and 285/40 x 17in items at the rear.

Superbly designed, the Oxia was a realistic proposition. The usual duo from the Peugeot styling department, Gérard Welter for the exterior and Paul Bracq for the interior, came up with a highly desirable vehicle. Its lines (drawn up by E Berthot) were taut, the volumes ideally proportioned and stamped with the marque's identity. The cockpit reflected the technology with a mix of steel-grey

and strong blues, melding leather and a dark aluminium. The car seemed ready to take to the track, so much did it conform to the image of a true GT. The body was made of carbon-fibre and kevlar, epoxy-glued to an aluminium honeycomb structure; CdA was 0.63 and Cd 0.32.

The engine was mid-mounted, set transversely. It was a twin-turbo V6, with twin overhead camshafts per bank and four valves per cylinder. With a capacity of 2,849cc, it developed 680bhp at 8,200rpm and a maximum torque of 535lb ft at 4,500rpm. There was a six-speed gearbox, and both four-wheel drive and four-wheel steering.

PEUGEOT OXIA

In full supercar euphoria, people dreamt that the Peugeot Oxia could be a rival to the Ferrari F40, Porsche 959 and Jaguar XJ-220.

CITROËN ACTIVA (D3)

CITROËN ACTIVA (D3)

CITROËN ACTIVA (D3) Paris, September 1988. Four-door saloon (Cd 0.25) conceived under the direction of Art Blakeslee. 4wd and four-wheel steering, hydraulic/electronic sususpension. Engine: 3-litre V6. Power: 220bhp. Length: 475cm. Width: 190cm. Height: 127cm.

RENAULT MÉGANE (G-STUDIO)

CADILLAC VOYAGE

CADILLAC VOYAGE New York, January 1988. With its show 'GM Teamwork and Technology for Today and Tomorrow' General Motors recreated the atmosphere of the 1950s Motoramas, in the setting of the Waldorf Astoria – where they presented the Chevrolet Venture, Pontiac Banshee, Buick Lucerne, GMC Centaur and Cadillac Voyage. The Cadillac was a luxury saloon (Cd 0.28) with countless electronic 'assistances'. Engine: 4,467cc V8. Power: 279bhp. Length: 540cm. Width: 198cm. Height: 136cm. Wheelbase: 304cm. Weight: 1,725cm.

RENAULT MÉGANE (G-STUDIO) Paris, October 1988. Saloon (Cd 0.21) with four sliding doors and a bubble back with the rear window sliding back and forth to increase interior space. First concept car at Renault created under the direction of Patrick Le Quément (with Jean-François Venet). Four-wheel drive and electronically-controlled suspension. Engine: 2,965cc V6. Power: 250bhp at 6,000rpm. Length: 495cm. Width: 190cm. Height: 142cm. Weight: 1,800kg.

PLYMOUTH SLINGSHOT

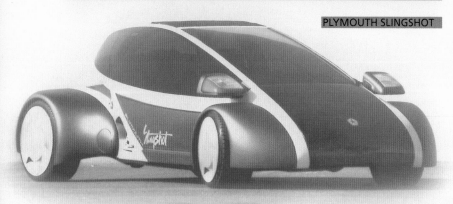

AUDI ASGARD (ITAL DESIGN)

AUDI ASGARD (ITAL DESIGN) Turin, April 1988. Using the same architecture (mid-mounted transverse Audi 200 engine), Ital Design developed three different vehicles: the Aztec roadster, the Aspid coupé, and the sporting 'monospace' Asgard. Length: 441.5cm. Width: 197cm. Height: 157.5cm. Wheelbase: 290cm.

PLYMOUTH SLINGSHOT Los Angeles, January 1988. Mid-engined fun coupé, designed under the direction of Thomas C Gale, Chrysler design chief since 1985. Engine: 2.2-litre dohc 16v twin-turbo 4-cyl. Length: 378.3cm. Width: 172.8cm. Height: 121.1cm. Wheelbase: 261.5cm.

FORD SAGUARO (GHIA) Geneva, March 1988. Four-door seven-seater compact all-terrain vehicle with high ground clearance. Created by Giuseppe Delena, this premonitory project (Cd 0.29) laid down a new design direction for 4x4s. The Saguro was exhibited at the Maison de Radio France as part of the April/May 1989 exhibition 'Des voitures et des hommes'. Length: 432.1. Width: 169.6. Height: 136.9cm.

FORD SAGUARO (GHIA)

LANCIA HIT (PININFARINA)

LAMBORGHINI GENESIS (BERTONE)

LANCIA HIT (PININFARINA) Turin, April 1988. Coupé (Cd 0.29) based on the Delta Integrale and exploring the intensive use of composite materials – sandwich construction of honeycomb Nomex panels and carbon-fibre panels resulted in a platform weighing only 40kg. Created under the direction of Lorenzo Ramaciotti, in charge of Pininfarina's *Studi e Ricerche* from 1988. Engine: 1,995cc 4-cyl. Power: 185bhp at 5,300rpm. Length: 397cm. Width: 172cm. Height: 132cm. Wheelbase: 247.5cm.

LAMBORGHINI GENESIS (BERTONE) Turin, April 1988. Grand touring five-seater one-box vehicle dreamt up by Marc Deschamps (exterior) and Eugenio Pagliano (interior). Mid-mounted Lamborghini power unit and automatic transmission. Engine: 3,929cc V12. Power: 350bhp at 7,500rpm. Length: 447.5cm. Width: 200cm. Height: 152cm. Wheelbase: 265cm.

ISUZU 4200R

FERRARI MYTHOS (PININFARINA)

ISUZU 4200 R Tokyo, November 1989. Mid-engined four-seater coupé which bore witness to the links between Isuzu and Lotus: active suspension by Lotus. Design by Julian Thomson under the direction of Shiro Nakamura. Engine: 4.2-litre dohc 32v V8. Length: 463cm. Width: 191cm. Height: 135cm. Wheelbase: 263cm.

FERRARI MYTHOS (PININFARINA) Tokyo, November 1989. Mid-engined roadster based on the Ferrari Testarossa. The design, by Piero Camardella working under Lorenzo Ramaciotti, was marked by a considerable effort to integrate efficient aerodynamics – Cd 0.27 – with the styling themes. Engine: 4,942cc flat-12. Power: 390bhp at 6,300rpm. Length: 430.5cm. Width: 211cm. Height: 106.5cm. Wheelbase: 255cm. Weight: 1,250kg.

MATRA M25 (D3)

SUZUKI CONSTELLATION

MATRA M25 (D3) Nîmes, April 1989. Renault-powered fun car intended to offer impressive acceleration; designed by Aimé Saugues and created to celebrate 25 years of Matra. Engine: 1,764cc dohc 16v turbo 4-cyl. Power: 200bhp at 5,500rpm. Maximum torque: 198lb ft at 4,500rpm. Length: 347cm. Width: 174cm. Height: 122cm. Wheelbase: 243cm. Weight: 700kg, giving 3.5kg per bhp.

SUZUKI CONSTELLATION Tokyo, November 1989. All-terrain 4wd estate with four-wheel steering and variable ground clearance; monocoque construction. Multi-function audio system. Engine: 3-litre 24v V6. Power: 220bhp at 6,500rpm. Length: 419.5cm. Width: 185.5cm. Height: 185.5cm. Wheelbase: 257cm. Weight: 1,650kg.

PONTIAC STINGER

FORD VIA (GHIA)

PONTIAC STINGER Detroit, January 1989. Four-wheel-drive leisure vehicle in keeping with the trends of the time – Plymouth's Speedster and Ford's Splash were in the same spirit. Engine: Twin-cam 16v 4-cyl. Power: 172bhp at 6,500rpm. Length: 419cm. Width: 187cm. Height: 149cm. Wheelbase: 149cm.

FORD VIA (GHIA) Geneva, March 1989. Sporting four-door saloon designed by Claudio Messale. First car in the world to be fitted with fibre-optic headlamps. Transparent roof in photo-sensitive glass. Transverse turbocharged V8 mated to six-speed gearbox; four-wheel drive. Length: 445.9cm. Width: 192cm. Height: 126cm. Wheelbase: 279.4cm.

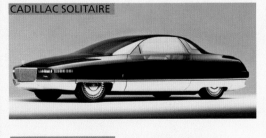

CADILLAC SOLITAIRE

IAD VENUS Tokyo, November 1989. Futuristic mid-engined coupé designed by Michael Arni and based on the Lotus Esprit. Engine: 2,174cc dohc 16v 4-cyl. Power: 174bhp at 6,500rpm. Maximum torque: 163lb ft at 5,000rpm. Length: 400cm. Width: 195cm. Height: 111cm. Wheelbase: 269.5cm.

CADILLAC SOLITAIRE Detroit, January 1989. Luxurious aerodynamic (Cd 0.28) coupé with engine developed in conjunction with Lotus; rear-wheel-drive, automatic transmission. Engine: 6.6-litre dohc 48v V12. Power: 430bhp. Length: 544.1cm. Width: 198.6cm. Height: 137.8cm. Wheelbase: 303.8cm.

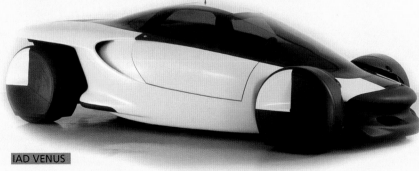

IAD VENUS

THE IDEA OF REVIVING ALPINE HAS OFTEN PREOCCUPIED RENAULT'S DESIGNERS. IT COULD HAVE COME TO SOMETHING CONCRETE WITH THE LAGUNA ROADSTER, BUT IN THE END THE CAR'S ONLY LEGACY WAS THE NAME IT PASSED ON TO RENAULT'S MID-RANGER.

RENAULT LAGUNA (D3)

aris, October 1990. Patrick Le Quément took over the reins of Renault's Industrial Design department in January 1988. Then 43 years old, Le Quément had benefited from a British education and was a graduate of Birmingham Polytechnic. He began his career at Simca in 1966, then in the following year founded the Design International studio with John Pinko. He worked for a long time for Ford, at first (1968) in Cologne, then at Dunton in Britain (1976). Made responsible for advanced design at Merkenich, he became lieutenant to Uwe Bahnsen in 1979. After this for a short period (1985–87) he ran an advanced-design studio in Düsseldorf for the Volkswagen group.

Among the first initiatives Patrick Le Quément took on his arrival at the head of Renault's design department was to promote the creation of concept cars, something that had previously only happened from time to time. The Z02 project was launched from the advanced-design studio run by Jean-François Venet. The brief was for a sporting fun-car that was supposed to evoke the Alpine.

The design was the work of Jean-Pierre Ploué, fresh from the ENSAAMA, where he had received a degree in interior architecture. Ian Matthews was responsible for the interior. The style mixed purity and complexity, and was sensual without falling into the traps of bio-design. For the colour schemes Sophie Milenovic drew her inspiration from the palette of David Hockney, one of Patrick Le Quément's favourite painters…

The dimensions of the Laguna were a length of 411.4cm, a width of 183.2cm and a height of 98.9cm, the whole built on a 351.5cm wheelbase. The body was built by D3, a firm created in 1988 by Bernard Pène, who had previously been a model-maker at Renault for 13 years.

The wishbone suspension and the tubular chassis were specially developed for the prototype, but the 2-litre engine, mated to a five-speed gearbox, came from the Renault 21 Turbo. The 1,995cc unit developed 210bhp at 5,500rpm, with maximum torque of 152lb ft at 3,000rpm.

The Laguna wasn't particularly light, at 900kg; it sat on 205/45 x 18in rubber at the front and 235/40R x 18in tyres at the rear. With a CdA of 0.64, a maximum speed of 150mph was envisaged.

The Laguna used a one-off chassis based around a mid-engined layout. The styling was still clearly influenced by the fashion for bio-design.

FORD SHOCCCWAVE

OLDSMOBILE EXPRESSION Detroit, January 1990.
Elegantly streamlined estate which envisaged an evolution of
the US station wagon towards a more sporting style. Engine:
2,260cc Quad 4 turbo 4-cyl. Power: 230bhp. Length: 509cm.
Width: 189cm. Height: 140cm. Wheelbase: 266.5cm.

FORD SHOCCCWAVE Paris, October 1990. Front-engined two-seater coupé in very conventional style, with soft
and banal lines. In fact, not really shocking at all…

CHEVROLET CERV III

Detroit, January 1990.
Two-seater mid-engined
GT, and yet another
attempt to come up with a
new architecture for the
Corvette. Composite body;
carbon-fibre backbone
chassis designed by Lotus;
four-wheel steering.
Engine: 5.7-litre LT-5 twin-
turbo V8. Power: 650bhp
at 6,000rpm. Length:
491.7cm. Width: 203.2cm.
Height: 114.8cm.
Wheelbase: 247.9cm.
Weight: 1,542kg.

CHEVROLET CERV III

FORD ZIG / ZAG (GHIA)

CHEVROLET NIVOLA (BERTONE)

CHEVROLET NIVOLA (BERTONE) Geneva, March 1990. Mid-engined two-seater GT
with ZR-1 Corvette engine. Way Assauto hydropneumatic suspension; chassis created
with Nova Progetti and Albatech. Length: 420.5cm. Width: 198cm. Height: 110cm.

CITROËN SCARABÉE D'OR (HEULIEZ) Geneva,
March 1990. Compact off-road prototype using Citroën
mechanicals. The name paid tribute to one of the Citroën
half-tracks from the 1922–23 crossing of the Sahara.
Engine: 1,905cc 4-cyl. Power: 107bhp. Length: 320cm.

PONTIAC SUNFIRE

FORD ZIG / ZAG (GHIA) Geneva, March 1990. Two
complementary Fiesta-based studies: the Zig, a roadster
designed by Claudio Messale, and the Zag, a fun van
created by David Wilkie. In May 1991 the Zag was given
an Orbital two-stroke engine. Length: 354.5cm (Zig)/
338.9cm (Zag). Wheelbase: 223cm.

CITROËN ACTIVA 2

PONTIAC SUNFIRE

Detroit, January 1990.
Very pretty 2+2 coupé with
two main doors and two
smaller suicide-hinged rear
doors. Other GM concept
cars unveiled at Detroit
were the Cadillac Aurora
and the Buick Bolero.
Engine: 2-litre 16v turbo 4-
cyl. Power: 190bhp.
Maximum torque:
205lb ft at 6,000rpm.
Length: 455cm.
Wheelbase: 277cm.

CITROËN SCARABÉE D'OR (HEULIEZ)

CITROËN ACTIVA 2 Paris, October 1990. Four-seater
coupé with 'hydractive' suspension incorporating
automatic levelling and an active anti-roll system; four-
speed automatic transmission. Styled by Dan Abramson,
under Art Blakeslee. Engine: 2,975cc 24v V6. Power:
200bhp at 6,000rpm.

AUDI AVUS QUATTRO

AUDI AVUS QUATTRO Tokyo, October 1991. After the Quattro Spyder (Frankfurt 1991), this mid-engined 4wd aluminium GT paid tribute to the 1937 Auto-Union record-breaker. Designed under Hartmut Warkuss, head of Audi design from 1976 until 1993. Engine: 5,998cc W12. Power: 509bhp at 5,800rpm. Maximum torque: 399lb ft at 4,000rpm. Gearbox: six-speed. Length: 442.4cm. Width: 197.6cm. Height: 117.4cm. Wheelbase: 280cm. Weight: 1,250kg. Maximum speed: 211mph.

PONTIAC PROTOSPORT4

PONTIAC PROTOSPORT4 Detroit, January 1991. Sporting four-door saloon with front-mounted V8, designed by John Manoogian (exterior) and Bill Scott (interior). Also at Detroit were the Ford Contour, the General Motors HX3 and the Mercedes-Benz F100.

LOTUS EMOTION (BERTONE)

LOTUS EMOTION (BERTONE) Detroit, January 1991. Mid-engined GT based on the Lotus Esprit. Elegant and taut style created under the direction of Marc Deschamps; also shown at Geneva. Length: 406cm. Width: 190cm. Height: 108cm. Wheelbase: 245cm.

RENAULT SCÉNIC

RENAULT SCÉNIC Frankfurt, September 1991. Compact 4wd 'monospace' whose concept anticipated the production Mégane Scénic; designed by Anne Asencio under Patrick le Quément. A thick perimeter chassis aided rigidity and provided stowage facilities. Engine: 1,964cc F7R 16v 4-cyl. Power: 150bhp at 6,000rpm. Maximum torque: 141lb ft at 3,500rpm. Length: 415cm. Width: 192cm. Height: 185cm. Wheelbase: 275cm. Weight: 1,415kg. Maximum speed:113mph.

CHRYSLER 300

Detroit, January 1991. This impressive sports saloon with its 8-litre V10 mined the post-modernism seam with its OSCA-style grille and feline lines. Designed under Neil Walling at Chrysler Pacifica. At the same show Chrysler exhibited the Dodge Neon and the Jeep Wagoneer 2000.

NISSAN TRI-X Tokyo, October 1991. Four-seater coupé aimed at the protection of the environment. 4,494cc VHX V8 engine (dohc 32v) develops 334bhp on 85% methanol and 15% petrol. Length: 499.5cm. Width: 190cm. Height: 135cm. Wheelbase: 280cm.

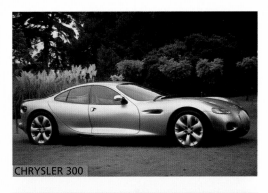

CHRYSLER 300

NISSAN TRI-X

BMW NAZCA C2 (ITAL DESIGN)

BMW NAZCA C2 (ITAL DESIGN) Tokyo, October 1991. Mid-engined GT following on from the Nazca M12 (Geneva 1991); running gear and carbon-fibre chassis designed at Ital Design under the supervision of Fabrizio Giugiaro. The spider C2 would be shown at the opening of the Monaco Grand Prix in May 1992. Engine: 5,660cc V12. Power: 380bhp. Length: 436.5cm. Width: 199cm. Height: 110.5cm. Wheelbase: 260cm. Weight: 1000kg.

OPELCHRONOS (PININFARINA)

OPELCHRONOS (PININFARINA) Detroit, January 1991. Front-engined roadster based on the bulky mechanicals of the Opel Omega Lotus (Vauxhall Lotus Carlton). Engine: 3,615cc twin-turbo 6-cyl. Power: 377bhp at 5,200rpm. Length: 432cm. Width: 188cm. Height: 125cm. Wheelbase: 245cm.

THE CORVETTE NEVER STOPS MAKING DESIGNERS DREAM. FOR THEM IT IS AN INEXHAUSTIBLE THEME BASED ON THE DEFENCE AND THE ILLUSTRATION OF A CERTAIN AUTOMOTIVE HERITAGE. WATCH OUT – MASTERPIECE AHEAD!

CHEVROLET CORVETTE STING RAY III

Detroit, January 1992. All that remains of the American Dream must be preserved: that was the view of Chuck Jordan, 1986–92 vice-president in charge of design at General Motors. Hollywood designer and Ferrari fan, he never strayed from this conviction.

It was in this spirit that the Corvette Sting Ray III was born. It was developed in California, by the General Motors Advanced Concepts Center at Thousand Oaks, 30 miles from Los Angeles. Founded in September 1983, the studio was successively run by Henry Haga, John Schinella, and finally – from 1992 – by Terry Henline, all three important personalities in the world of American design.

The Sting Ray III was developed during Schinella's reign. Nicknamed 'The California Corvette', the Sting Ray III brought with it a completely fresh take on the traditional Corvette. It was a purified, contemporary, aggressive interpretation, devoid of compromise. Although the wheelbase was longer than that of the production Corvette, the Sting Ray III was shorter overall and visually more dynamic: it was 443.2cm long, 188.7cm wide, and 106.7cm high, on a 261.6cm wheelbase that was extended by 17cm relative to the production car.

After the numerous projects for a mid-engined Corvette, this time the classic engine configuration was promoted, with the Sting Ray III powered by a Corvette LT1 engine mounted at the front.

Built in the course of 1991, the Corvette Sting Ray III was finally one of the big stars of the 1992 Detroit Autoshow. There it rubbed shoulders with the Buick Sceptre, the Chevrolet Sizigi, the Oldsmobile Anthem and the Pontiac Salsa from General Motors, as well as the Ford Connecta (Ghia) and the Lincoln Marque X from the number two of the Big Three, and the Cirrus from Chrysler.

The Sting Ray III, more sensual and more compact than the production Corvette, suddenly made it look old hat. This 'California Corvette' was the work of the Thousand Oaks studio near Los Angeles.

PININFARINA ETHOS

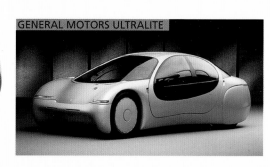

GENERAL MOTORS ULTRALITE

PININFARINA ETHOS

Turin, April 1992.
Simplified sporting roadster with a clear continuity between the interior and exterior styling; designer Stephan Schwartz. Aluminium structure by Hydro Aluminium Automotive, with plastic body by GE Plastics. Engine: 1.2-litre two-stroke Orbital. Power: 95bhp. Maximum torque: 92lb ft. Length: 363cm. Width: 166cm. Height: 105cm. Wheelbase: 230cm. Weight: 700kg.

HEULIEZ RAFFICA

Paris, October 1992. First creation of the Heuliez Torino studio set up in 1992 by Marc Deschamps (ex-Renault, ex-Bertone, ex-Coggiola). This roadster – an un-motorised mock-up – inherited his innate sense of proportion and sculpture. Length: 420cm. Width: 190cm. Height: 124cm. Wheelbase: 250cm.

FORD FOCUS (GHIA)

ITAL DESIGN COLUMBUS

OPEL TWIN

Geneva, March 1992. Prototype based on the concept of interchangeable rear-mounted power-unit modules – either 34bhp three-cylinder petrol engine or two 14bhp three-phase electric motors. Front suspension by plastic transverse leaf spring. Length: 347cm. Width: 163cm. Height: 136cm. Weight: 540kg (petrol) or 740kg (batteries).

FORD FOCUS (GHIA)

Turin, April 1992.
Roadster based on Escort RS Cosworth. The cockpit mixed wood decking and Mexican saddle-leather; designer Taru Lahti. Engine: 1,994cc turbo 4-cyl. Power: 220bhp. Length: 413.5cm. Width: 179.3cm. Height: 122.4cm. Weight: 950kg.

ITAL DESIGN COLUMBUS

Turin, April 1992.
Impressive 'voyager', developed as a counterpoint to the 500th anniversary of the discovery of America by Christopher Columbus. Powered by a mid-mounted BMW engine, it carried seven people in its limousine configuration. Four-wheel drive and four-wheel steering. Engine: 5-litre V12. Power: 300bhp. Length: 599.7cm. Width: 219cm. Height: 206cm. Wheelbase: 382cm.

GENERAL MOTORS ULTRALITE

Detroit, January 1992. Saloon reconciling lightness and aerodynamic efficiency (Cd 0.192), built around a carbon-fibre body composed of only six elements and weighing only 210kg. Rear-mounted two-stroke power unit. Engine: 1.5-litre 3-cyl. Power: 111bhp at 4,500rpm. Maximum torque: 123lb ft at 4,000rpm. Length: 420.6cm. Width: 162.5cm. Height: 129.1cm. Wheelbase: 279.4cm. Weight: 700kg.

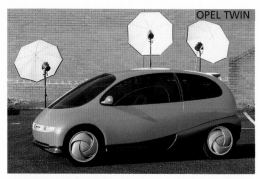

OPEL TWIN

RENAULT ZOOM (MATRA)

RENAULT ZOOM (MATRA)

Paris, October 1992. Electric two-seater urban vehicle (range 90 miles) conceived by Matra Automobile under Georges Héroguelle. The car – which was plastic-bodied – could be made more compact for parking, thanks to its variable wheelbase. Power unit: 25kW electric motor; nickel-cadmium batteries. Length: 230/265cm. Width: 152cm. Height: 149.5/172.5cm. Wheelbase: 124.5/184.5cm. Weight: 800kg.

LANCIA MAGIA (IAD)

LANCIA MAGIA (IAD)

Turin, April 1992. Coupé based on the 4wd Lancia Dedra Integrale, designed by Michael Ani under Alan Jackson. Engine: 2-litre turbo 4-cyl. Power: 178bhp at 5,250rpm. Length: 420cm. Width: 176.3cm. Height: 130.2cm. Wheelbase: 254cm.

HEULIEZ RAFFICA

FORD SUB'B

ASTON MARTIN LAGONDA VIGNALE (GHIA)

FORD SUB'B Frankfurt, September 1983. City car characterised by its lack of bumper-shields. Rear-mounted 1.2-litre 82bhp two-stroke. Length: 340cm. Width: 164cm. Height: 150cm. Wheelbase: 237cm.

RENAULT RACOON

BUGATTI EB 112 (ITAL DESIGN)

ASTON MARTIN LAGONDA VIGNALE (GHIA)
Geneva, March 1993. Saloon with a nostalgic flavour, featuring an interior of Art Deco inspiration (grey beech-wood and nickel). Engine: 60 degree V12 (two Duratec V6s joined together). Power: 400bhp at 5,000rpm. Maximum torque: 399lb ft at 4,500rpm. Length: 523.6cm. Width: 195.5cm. Height: 144.9cm. Wheelbase: 311.8cm.

RENAULT RACOON Geneva, March 1993. All-terrain amphibious 4wd three-seater inspired by the design language of the helicopter and the construction-site vehicle. Styled by Axel Breün under the direction of Patrick Le Quément. Engine: mid-mounted 2,963cc V6. Power: 262bhp at 6,000rpm. Maximum torque: 268lb ft at 2,500rpm. Six-speed gearbox. Length: 411cm. Width: 180cm. Height: 211.5cm. Wheelbase: 257.7cm. Weight: 1,580kg. Maximum speed: 96mph.

BUGATTI EB 112 (ITAL DESIGN) Geneva, March 1993. Two-box grand-touring saloon. The central rib on the roof and the radiator grille recall the Bugatti Atlantic. Engine: 6-litre V12. Power: 455bhp at 6,300rpm. Maximum torque: 434lb ft at 3,000rpm. Length: 507cm. Width: 196cm. Height: 140.5cm. Wheelbase: 310cm. Weight: 1,800kg.

SUBARU SAGRES

ISUZU XU-1 (METALCRAFTERS)

NISSAN AP-X Tokyo, November 1993. Front-engined coupé ('AP' is for 'Attractive Performer') which served as launchpad for a new compact lightweight engine; design by Marcello Gandini. Engine: 3-litre 24v VQ-X dohc V6. Power: 250bhp at 7,000rpm. Maximum torque: 217lb ft at 5,200rpm.

SUBARU SAGRES Tokyo, November 1993. As a follow-up to the SRD concept car of 1989, Subaru explored the idea of a streamlined sporting one-box design that blurred the line between saloon and estate. 2-litre flat-four. Power: 203bhp. Four-wheel drive. Length: 433cm. Width: 177cm. Height: 131cm. Wheelbase: 277cm.

NISSAN AP-X

BMW Z13

ISUZU XU-1 (METALCRAFTERS) Tokyo, November 1993. Sporting luxury off-road estate which heralded the development of the 'Sports Utility Vehicle' or SUV. Designed by Californian studio ITCA. Engine: 3.2-litre V6. Length: 446cm. Width: 179cm. Height: 160cm. Wheelbase: 276cm.

BMW Z13 Geneva, March 1993. Interesting study for a three-seater coupé with central driving position and two rear-set passenger seats; led to the E1 prototypes shown at Frankfurt in 1991 and 1993. Conceived by BMW Technik under Klaus Kapitza. Engine: 1.1-litre mid-mounted K1100RS 4-cyl. Power: 82bhp. CVT transmission. Length: 344cm. Width: 164cm. Height: 132cm. Weight: 730kg.

RENAULT WAS WORLD CHAMPION F1 CONSTRUCTOR SIX TIMES BETWEEN 1992 AND 1997. TO CELEBRATE THIS EXTRAORDINARY DOMINANCE, IT CAME UP WITH A MADCAP CONCEPT CAR…

Paris, October 1994. In 1994 Renault celebrated its third consecutive victory in the F1 constructors' championship, and the third achieved in association with Williams. As an exercise in provocation Renault devised a wonderfully lunatic prototype.

Renault had sufficient panache to thumb its nose at the grimness of the time by forgetting – for as long as the dream lasted – all notions of commonsense and reason, and the company's economic and financial travails. To celebrate the tenth birthday of its most rational production model – the Espace – Renault decided to produce the most provocative vehicle in its history. An incredible MPV was developed, using the mechanicals of a Formula 1 single-seater. An RS4 engine (as used in the 1992 season) sat in the middle of this machine, known until then as a rolling tribute to convivial motoring…

Thanks to its 3.5-litre V10, the Espace F1 whisked its four occupants to 120mph in only 6.3 seconds. Maximum speed was estimated at 180mph. The engineers at Williams, who were Renault's partners in Grand Prix racing, provided the rear running gear and checked over the front end, while Matra Automobile was tasked with bringing some coherence to this improbable high-octane cocktail.

The silhouette of the MPV was still evident, but the enlarged wings housed huge tyres, a huge air-scoop dominated the front end, and a hard-to-miss spoiler was fitted above the rear tailgate.

The interior made substantial use of carbon-fibre, a material mastered to perfection by the Moc company run by Philippe Moch and part of the Rhône-Poulenc group.

RENAULT ESPACE F1 (MATRA)

This joyful prototype reconciled two facets of Renault's reputation: its victorious participation in Formula 1 and its engagement in the MPV market with the Espace.

At the same time as the Espace F1, Renault unveiled the Ludo small car, the Modus van, and the Amératrice city-car mock-ups.

Under the familiar silhouette of the Renault Espace MPV hide the mechanicals of a Formula 1 car. Williams and Matra played a big part in the construction of this prototype.

FIORAVANTI SENSIVA

PORSCHE KARISMA (BERTONE)

DP BARRAMUNDA

Paris, October 1994. Sporting coupé with built-in jet-ski and surfboards. The engines lodged in the side pods were BMW motorcycle units. The design was the work of Eric de Pauw, founder of Design Performance.

PORSCHE KARISMA (BERTONE) Geneva, March 1994. Two-door four-seater saloon with a rear-mounted Porsche 911 engine hanging out behind the rear axle. The design was created under Luciano d'Ambrosio, head of Bertone's styling department from 1992 until 1999. Engine: Porsche flat-six. Length: 452cm. Width: 186cm. Height: 134.5cm.

RENAULT ARGOS (G-STUDIO)

RENAULT ARGOS (G-STUDIO) Geneva, March 1994. Minimalist three-seater roadster based on the Twingo. Designed by Jean-Pierre Ploué under Jean-François Venet and Patrick Le Quément, it initiated a style called 'Esprit Nouveau' which broke with bio-design and which would be exploited on the Clio. Engine: 1,239cc 4-cyl. Length: 378cm. Width: 172cm. Height: 110cm. Wheelbase: 234.7cm. Weight: 750kg.

PININFARINA ETHOS 3 Turin, April 1994. A compact six-seater saloon, this was the third development of the Ethos line, following the spider (Turin 1992) and the Ethos 2 coupé (Geneva 1993); at the Los Angeles show in 1996 the electric-powered Ethos 3EV derivative was shown. The steering wheel and pedals could be moved at will from left to right. Engine: 3-cyl. Length: 324cm. Width: 169cm. Height: 147cm. Wheelbase: 230cm. Weight: 780kg.

FIORAVANTI SENSIVA

Turin, April 1994. Head of Pininfarina's *Centro Studi e Ricerche* from 1972 until 1988, deputy managing director of Ferrari from 1998 to 1990, then chief of Fiat's *Centro Stile* from 1990 to 1991, Leonardo Fioravanti founded his own company and used this coupé as his visiting card; it was powered by electric motors linked to a gas-turbine developing 230bhp at 100,000rpm. Length: 412cm. Width: 188cm. Height: 120cm. Wheelbase: 265cm. Weight: 1000kg. Maximum speed: 150mph.

CITROËN XANAE

DP BARRAMUNDA

LEXUS LANDAU (ITAL DESIGN)

LEXUS LANDAU (ITAL DESIGN) Geneva, March 1994. Two-box saloon based on the Lexus GS300. In cutting back the front and rear overhangs to the maximum, it was possible to arrive at a completely different and very compact expression of how a luxury car could be. Engine: 3,968cc 32v V8. Power: 260bhp. Length: 427cm.

PEUGEOT ION

CITROËN XANAE Paris, October 1994. This compact MPV, based on the Xantia Activa, anticipated the Xsara Picasso; designed by Mark Lloyd under Art Blakeslee. Engine: 2-litre 4-cyl. Power: 135bhp at 5,500rpm. Length: 423cm. Width: 180cm. Height: 155cm.

PEUGEOT ION Paris, October 1994. Electric vehicle conceived by PSA's centre of advanced design. The mechanicals were the work of Jean-Christophe Bolle-Reddat, the exterior was by Chris Cadman working under Curt Gwin, and the interior was created by Yves Dubernard. Power came from a 20kW electric motor powered by nickel-cadmium batteries. Length: 332cm. Width: 160cm. Height: 145cm. Weight: 850kg. Maximum speed: 65mph. Range: 70–90 miles.

PININFARINA ETHOS 3

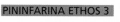

HYUNDAI HCD-III

CHRYSLER ATLANTIC (METALCRAFTERS)

CHRYSLER ATLANTIC (METALCRAFTERS) Detroit, January 1995. Hollywood-style neo-classic coupé; designed by Bob Hubbach under Tom Gale; presented at Detroit alongside the Eagle Jazz and the Plymouth Back Pack. Engine: 4-litre 32v 8-cyl (two Neon 4-cyl units joined together). Power: 325bhp. Length: 506.7cm. Width: 192.5cm. Height: 131.1cm. Wheelbase: 320cm.

FORD GT90

FORD GT90 Detroit, January 1995. Mid-engined GT which launched Ford's 'New Edge Design' with its juxtaposition of multiple diagonal intersections; created under the direction of Jack Telnack. Engine: 6-litre V12. Power: 720bhp. Maximum torque: 645lb ft. Wheelbase: 295cm. Other concept cars at Detroit included the Buick XP2000, Lincoln L2K, Oldsmobile Antares and Pontiac Grand Prix 300GPX.

RENAULT INITIALE (G-STUDIO)

HYUNDAI HCD-III Detroit, January 1995. Fusion between a coupé and an off-roader; design by Roger Flores of the Hyundai California Center. Four-wheel drive and variable ground clearance; five-speed gearbox. Engine: 2-litre 16v dohc turbo 4-cyl. Power: 240bhp at 6,100rpm. Maximum torque: 201lb ft at 4,700rpm. Length: 412.2cm. Width: 187.7cm. Height: 142.2cm/149.9cm. Wheelbase: 249.9cm.

LANCIA KAYAK (BERTONE)

LANCIA KAYAK (BERTONE) Geneva, March 1995. Intentionally conventional and realistic coupé based on the Lancia Kappa; this running prototype was again shown at Turin in 1996. Engine: 2,446cc 5-cyl. Length: 468cm. Width: 186cm. Height: 136cm. Wheelbase: 270cm.

OPEL MAXX Geneva, March 1995. City car proposed in various forms, with either a long or a short wheelbase; extruded aluminium hull. Designed under Richard Ruzzin, in charge from 1991 until 1996. Engine: 973cc Ecotec ohc 3-cyl. Power: 50bhp at 5,000rpm. Length: 297.5cm (2-dr) or 373cm (4-dr). Width: 157.5cm. Height: 157.5cm. Weight: 600kg.

RENAULT INITIALE (G-STUDIO) Frankfurt, September 1995. Luxury saloon based on the Safrane Turbo. Shown at the Bagatelle concours before its début at Frankfurt. Innovative design by Florian Thiercelin (exterior) and Fabio Filipini (interior), under Jean-François Venet. Built by G-Studio. Engine: 3.5-litre RS6 turbo V10. Power: 392bhp at 8,000rpm. Maximum torque: 266lb ft at 6,200rpm. Length: 488.1cm. Width: 199.5cm. Height: 144.3cm. Wheelbase: 302cm. Weight: 1,950kg.

BMW JUST 4/2 Tokyo, November 1995. Minimalist fun car borrowing both its design language and its engine from the world of motorcycles. Engine: Dohc 4-cyl. Power: 100bhp at 7,500rpm. Weight: 500kg. 0–60mph in 6 seconds.

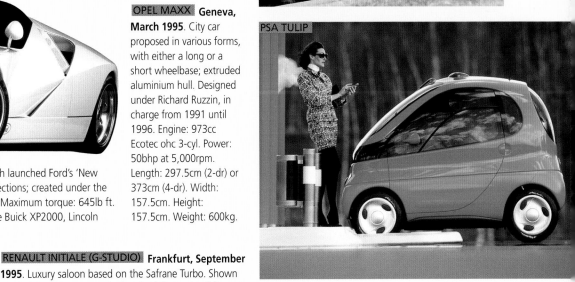
BMW JUST 4/2

OPEL MAXX

PSA TULIP

PSA TULIP Paris, March 1995. Original system of town transport with a network of electric vehicles on hire, a central office to run the network – from reservations to maintenance of the vehicles – and an infrastructure consisting of stops equipped with recharging posts. Users would be subscribers to the system and would have a personal hand-set. Length: 220cm. Width: 140cm. Height: 160cm.

LINCOLN MADE ITS CONTRIBUTION TO THE POST-MODERNIST MOVEMENT VIA A PROJECT THAT BLENDED NOSTALGIA AND MODERNITY WITH PRAISEWORTHY MASTERLINESS IN A HYMN TO THE '62 CONTINENTAL.

Detroit, January 1996. The Sentinel appeared at the Detroit show as a mock-up. It was black, troubling and monstruous, as sombre as a menace. The style was trumpeted as the 'New Edge Design' initiated by French designer Claude Lobo. In reality the Lincoln's sharp ribs and tautly delineated volumes were sourced more in the past than in any new artistic doctrine. The inspiration for the Sentinel was nothing other than the 1962 model-year Continental, masterpiece of masterpieces in the history of Lincoln. The long

flanks, smooth and flowing, bulging out at the sills and tucking in at the waistline, the immense 20in wheels emphasised by their swollen wheelarches, the prow flanked by two lines of whalebone, the beltline defined by a strip of chrome, the flattened passenger compartment sitting between the wings…these were all references which built a bridge between the future and the past.

The Sentinel was created by Ford's advanced design studio in Dearborn, run by Claude Lobo under the direction of Jack Telnack, vice-president of Ford

Corporate Design. After the lure of Detroit, Ford gave a dose of consistency to this object of pleasure: in August 1996 it reappeared in the form of a running prototype, on the lawns of Pebble Beach. A few weeks later, the Sentinel made its European début at the September 1996 *Automobiles Classiques* and Louis Vuitton Concours at Bagatelle in Paris.

The prototype had evolved relative to the original project; it was the work of Ghia, whose name was henceforth attached to the car, which was now called the Sentinel Ghia.

LINCOLN SENTINEL (GHIA)

The 1962 Continental was the inspiration for the Lincoln Sentinel. But when it was being conceived, Claude Lobo also showed his young stylists a Facel II…

Painted in a mouse-like grey, less sober than the black in which it had first taken to the stage, the Sentinel Ghia was less bulky than the original: its length was limited (!) to 530cm, its width to 191.2cm and its height to 134.2cm.

The intended engine was a 5,935cc V12 derived from that of the Indigo, but the prototype ran thanks to a Jaguar V12.

The objective of the Lincoln Sentinel was to put the shine back on a prestigious badge. Without a doubt the operation was a success.

ALFA ROMEO NUVOLA

ALFA ROMEO NUVOLA **Paris, October 1996.** Two-seater coupé, post-modern in style, designed under the direction of Walter da'Silva. Engine: 2.5-litre twin-turbo V6. Power: 300bhp. Length: 428.6cm. Wheelbase: 260cm.

PEUGEOT ASPHALTE

MERCEDES-BENZ F200 IMAGINATION (STOLA)

MERCEDES-BENZ F200 IMAGINATION (STOLA)

Paris, October 1996. Luxurious coupé by Mercedes-Benz Design of Japan, directed by Olivier Boulay under the command of Bruno Sacco, head of Mercedes design from 1974 until 1998. The work of Anthony Lo, and built by Stola in Turin. Length: 510.5cm. Wheelbase: 294.5cm.

FORD INDIGO

FORD INDIGO **Detroit, January 1996.** Very stripped-down roadster designed by Mark Adams (exterior) and John Hartnell (interior), under the direction of Claude Lobo, in charge of the Ford Advanced Design Division. The chassis was developed by Reynard Racing Cars Ltd (along the lines of its Indy racers). Cosworth 6-litre V12 engine based on the Duratec. Power: 435bhp at 6,100rpm. Maximum torque: 405lb ft at 5,250rpm. Sequential six-speed gearbox. Length: 445.5cm. Width: 205.1cm. Height: 100cm. Wheelbase: 289.5cm.

PEUGEOT ASPHALTE

Paris, October 1996. Simple fun roadster with a very narrow (73cm) rear track and 90bhp Peugeot 106 power. Designed under Gérard Welter, and presented at the same time as the interesting Touareg off-roader. Length: 343.5cm. Width: 178cm. Height: 103.5cm. Wheelbase: 230cm. Maximum speed: 120mph. 0–60mph: 9.5 seconds.

FIAT SONG (PININFARINA)

FIAT SONG (PININFARINA) **Turin, April 1996.** On the imposed theme of the Fiat Bravo/Brava, Pininfarina came up with a normal compact MPV for the road (Sing) and a more funky off-roader (Song). Length: 409.5cm. Width: 175.5cm. Height: 170cm. Wheelbase: 254cm.

RENAULT FIFTIE

Geneva, 1996. Two-seater coupé based on the aluminium structure of the Renault Sport Spider, and designed in a post-modern style by Benoît Jacob, under Patrick Le Quément (Study D3). It evoked the lines of the 4CV which was then celebrating its 50th birthday. Engine: mid-mounted ohc D7F 1,147cc 4-cyl. Power: 60bhp at 5,250rpm. Maximum torque: 69lb ft at 2,500rpm.

RENAULT FIFTIE

CNR ETABETA (PININFARINA)

CNR ETABETA (PININFARINA) **Turin, April 1996.** Modular small saloon (Cd 0.31) with a rear overhang capable of being extended by 22cm. Hybrid power: 1,108cc Fiat engine (66bhp) at the front and an electric motor at the rear. Length: 312cm/332cm. Width: 158cm. Height: 148cm. Wheelbase: 210cm. Weight: 1,300kg.

OPEL SLALOM (BERTONE) **Geneva, 1996.** 2+2 coupé based on the 2-litre 16v Opel Calibra. The orange livery was chosen in tribute to Veuve Clicquot champagne. Four-wheel drive. Length: 464.4cm. Width: 186cm. Height: 132cm. Wheelbase: 260cm.

OPEL SLALOM (BERTONE)

ALFA ROMEO SCIGHERA (ITAL DESIGN)

ALFA ROMEO SCIGHERA (ITAL DESIGN) **Geneva, March 1997**. Coupé with mid-mounted twin-turbo 3-litre Alfa Romeo V6 engine. Power: 400bhp at 7,500rpm. Six-speed gearbox ahead of the engine. Length: 432cm. Width: 198cm. Height: 114.5cm. Wheelbase: 260cm.

MERCURY MC4

CHRYSLER PHAETON (METALCRAFTERS)

CHRYSLER PHAETON (METALCRAFTERS) **Detroit, January 1997**. Impressive four-door tourer recalling the 1940s Chrysler Newport. Designed by Mark Trostle under the direction of John Herlitz and Tom Gale; other Chrysler concept cars at Detroit were the Dodge Copperhead and the Plymouth Pronto. Engine: 5.4-litre V12. Power: 425bhp. Length: 546.1cm. Width: 198.1cm. Height: 139.7cm. Wheelbase: 335.3cm.

HONDA JV-X

MERCURY MC4
Detroit, January 1997. Fine New Edge Style project for a four-door coupé, with the two smaller rear doors being of 'suicide' type. Designed by Marc Adams under Jack Telnack. Engine: 4.6-litre V8.

HONDA JV-X **Tokyo, November 1997**. Sporting one-box coupé equipped with the new 1-litre 'IMA' three-cylinder direct-injection VTEC engine. Length: 384cm. Width: 175cm. Height: 125.5cm. Wheelbase: 236cm.

JEEP ICON **Detroit, January 1997**. Brilliant interpretation of what an end-of century Jeep could be like; designed under the direction of Trevor Creed. Engine: 2.4-litre 4-cyl. Four-wheel drive. Length: 360.7cm. Width: 172cm. Height: 178.1cm. Wheelbase: 237.2cm.

CHRYSLER CCV

ROVER MINI ACV 30

JEEP ICON

ROVER MINI SPIRITUAL / SPIRITUAL TOO

MERCURY MC4

CHRYSLER CCV
Frankfurt, September 1997. Clever prototype reviving the spirit of the Citroën 2CV. Presented in autumn 1996 as the China Concept Vehicle, it became the Composite Concept Vehicle a year later. The CCV was made of a composite material derived from recycled plastic bottles. The number of assembly operations was reduced thanks to the small number of body panels used: two sets of two side panels incorporating the floor, the doors and the bumpers. Engine: 800cc 2-cyl. Weight: 544kg.

ROVER MINI ACV 30
Monaco, January 1997. Prototype created to celebrate the 30th anniversary of the third victory of the Mini-Cooper S in the Monte Carlo Rally (1964, 1965 and 1967). Based on the mid-engined 1.8-litre twin-cam MGF, and designed under BMW.

ROVER MINI SPIRITUAL / SPIRITUAL TOO **Geneva, March 1997**. Two linked projects that revisited the concept of the Issigonis-designed Mini. The Spiritual was a five-seater one-box saloon (310cm long and weighing 700kg) while the Spiritual Too was a more spacious development in the shape of a five-door saloon (350cm long and weighing 900kg). The three-cylinder 63bhp engine was mounted under the rear seat.

THE POST-MODERN (OR 'NEO-CLASSICAL') STYLE WAS A STRONG TREND IN CAR DESIGN AT THE END OF THE 20TH CENTURY. CHRYSLER IN PARTICULAR HAD RECOURSE TO THIS IMAGERY, MAKING REFERENCE TO THE LEGENDARY CLASSICS IN ITS HISTORY.

CHRYSLER CHRONOS (METALCRAFTERS)

Detroit, January 1998. The Chronos paid homage to the most flamboyant times in Chrysler design: it re-wrote, in a thoroughly contemporary language, the appropriately named 'Chrysler d'Elégance'.

The Chronos picked up on the excess and the design vocabulary of its illustrious ancestor: the aggressive prow with the thick cross-hatched and almost square grille, the headlamps recessed into cavities, the shouldered front wings and sculpted rears, the windows outlined by a vigorous curve.

It would be nice to be able to attribute this scrupulous exercise in style to a red-blooded American, but that wasn't the case. The designer of the Chronos is an inheritor of traditions of the Japanese artist Utamaro and the ritual flower arrangements known as *ikebana*. Born on 14 April 1955 in Osaka, Tokyo Fine Arts graduate Osamu Shikado left Planet Toyota in 1994 to join the team led by Tom Gale, in charge at Chrysler's design offices since 1985.

The rolling prototype was built by Metalcrafters on the wonderful mechanicals of the Dodge Viper, but with the V10 reduced in capacity from 8 litres to 6 litres while nonetheless delivering 350bhp.

The proportions of the Chronos were imposing, and the 21in wheels were in harmony with an overall length that stretched to over 17ft!

At the Detroit show Chrysler also displayed the Dodge Intrepid ESX-2 and the Plymouth Pronto Spider.

Magnificent, impressive, over-the-top, the Chrysler Chronos was a true dream car. Indeed, despite the unbridled extravagance of its dimensions this imposing saloon had a severely limited amount of room for four passengers.

BMW PICKSTER

BMW PICKSTER Geneva, March 1998. In response to the success of the pick-up in the US, Bertone imagined a sporting evolution of this type of bodywork. The design was created under the direction of Luciano d'Ambrosio (exterior) and Eugenio Pagliano (interior). Engine: 3.2-litre 24v 6-cyl. Power: 320bhp. Length: 483.3cm. Width: 197cm. Height: 136.5cm. Wheebase: 305.6cm.

FIORAVANTI F 100 (CECOMP) Turin, April 1998. GT coupé conceived by Leonardo Fioravanti to celebrate the 100th anniversary of the birth of Enzo Ferrari. A beautifully sculpted mock-up with no engine, though a mid-mounted V10 was envisaged; built by Cecomp. Length: 439cm. Width: 191cm. Height: 114cm. Wheelbase: 255cm.

AUDI STRUCTURA (ITAL DESIGN) Turin, April 1998. Sporting one-box design making references to Frank Lloyd Wright in its fusion of visible structural elements and exterior cladding; visibility was optimised. Engine: 5.6-litre Audi W12. Power: 420bhp. Length: 464cm. Width: 190cm. Height: 173cm. Wheelbase: 280cm.

JEEP JEEPSTER

AUDI STRUCTURA (ITAL DESIGN)

RENAULT VEL SATIS

JEEP JEEPSTER Detroit, January 1998. Hybrid vehicle uniting sporting coupé with off-roader, designed under Trevor Creed. Based on the Jeep Grand Cherokee, it had hydraulic suspension that allowed ground clearance to vary. Other concept cars at Detroit included the Buick Signia, Ford P2000 Diata, Karmann AFB Car, Lincoln Machete, Mitsubishi SST, Mobility Outfitters Gearbox and Pontiac Montana Thunder. Engine: 4.7-litre V8. Power: 275bhp.

RENAULT VEL SATIS Paris, October 1998. Four-seater coupé (Code Z09) which sought to give legitimacy to Renault as a producer of top-of-range cars. One-box volume structured by unrealistically sharp lines. Designed by Florian Thiercelin (exterior) and Dominique Marzloff (interior) under the direction of Jean-François Venet and Patrick Le Quément. Engine: 2,946cc 24v V6. Power: 210bhp. Length: 468cm. Width: 188cm. Height: 135cm. Wheelbase: 287.3cm.

JAGUAR XK 180

JAGUAR XK 180 Paris, September 1998. Roadster based on a shortened Jaguar XKR floorpan; aluminium body fashioned by Abbey Panels. Designed by Keith Helfet under Geoff Lawson (head of Jaguar styling 1984–1999) and built by the Special Vehicle Operations department. Engine: 4-litre twin-turbo V8. Power: 456bhp. Five-speed automatic gearbox.

LAMBORGHINI PREGUNTA (HEULIEZ)

ALFA ROMEO DARDO (PININFARINA)

LAMBORGHINI PREGUNTA (HEULIEZ) Paris, October 1998. Spectacular roadster based on Lamborghini Diablo mechanicals and created by Heuliez Torino under Marc Deschamps. Engine: 5,707cc mid-mounted V12. Power: 530bhp at 7,100rpm. Length: 451.6cm. Width: 208.4cm. Height: 110cm. Wheelbase: 265cm. Maximum speed: 207mph. 0–60mph: 4 seconds.

ALFA ROMEO DARDO (PININFARINA) Turin, April 1998. Roadster based on the Alfa Romeo 156. The style borrowed its arrowhead motif from the Alfa's grille. Engine: 2.5-litre V6. Power: 195cm. Length: 438.5cm. Width: 179.5cm. Height: 125cm. Wheelbase: 254cm.

BENTLEY HUNAUDIÈRES

ISUZU KAI

ISUZU KAI Tokyo, **November 1999**. Four-door off-roader designed by ITCE-Design (run by Atsuhiko Yamada, with Geoff Gardiner as designer). Based around two strong themes: architecture and tradition. The design language drew on traditional Japanese values: the front made reference to a *torii* (shrine gateway), the roof hinted at the curve of a bridge, while the lower quarters evoked the grids of *shoji* sliding screens, Engine: 3-litre direct-injection diesel V6. Four-wheel drive and automatic transmission. Length: 392cm. Width: 175cm. Height: 166cm. Wheelbase: 270cm.

BENTLEY HUNAUDIÈRES Geneva, March 1999. Mid-engined GT designed by Volkswagen's Wolfsburg design studio under Hartmut Warkuss. Engine: 8,004cc 72-degree W16. Power: 623bhp. Length: 443.2cm. Width: 198.5cm. Height: 119.2cm.

TOYOTA NCSV (D3)

BMW Z9

BMW Z9 Frankfurt, **September 1999**. Elegant coupé certain styling elements of which would be seen on the 2002 7-Series. Designed under Chris Bangle, by head of advanced design Thomas Plath; convertible version shown at 2000 Paris salon. Engine: 3.9-litre diesel V8. Length: 500cm. Wheelbase: 295cm.

PININFARINA METROCUBO

TOYOTA NCSV (D3) **Tokyo, November 1999**. Vehicle capable of being transformed from coupé to estate. Created by the EPOC studio in Brussels before the opening of the new ED2 European studio at Sophia Antipolis in May 2000. Engine: 1.8-litre 4-cyl. Length: 424cm. Width: 173.5cm. Height: 141cm. Wheelbase: 262cm.

BUGATTI EB18/3 CHIRON (ITAL DESIGN)

BUGATTI EB18/3 CHIRON (ITAL DESIGN) Frankfurt, **September 1999**. After the EB 118 coupé (Paris 1998) and the EB 218 saloon (Geneva 1999), Ital Design came back with this extraordinary carbon-fibre coupé. Engine: 6,255cc W18. Power: 555bhp. Maximum torque: 415lb ft. Length: 442cm. Width: 199.4cm. Height: 115cm.

CADILLAC EVOQ (METALCRAFTERS) Detroit, **January 1999**. Superb front-engined rear-drive two-seater coupé marking a new design orientation for Cadillac. Built on a Chevrolet Corvette platform, and designed by Kip Wasenko under Wayne Cherry. Engine: 4,228cc Northstar V8. Power: 405bhp at 6,400rpm. Maximum torque: 385lb ft at 4,000rpm. Length: 428.2cm. Width: 183.4cm. Height: 124.7cm. Wheelbase: 275.6cm.

PININFARINA METROCUBO Frankfurt, **September 1999**. Project for a town car, benefiting from Michelin's run-flat PAX System which did away with the need for a spare wheel. Four seats: three at the front and one crossways in the rear. Lombardini 35kW electric motor. Length: 258cm.

ALFA ROMEO BELLA (BERTONE)

CADILLAC EVOQ (METALCRAFTERS)

ALFA ROMEO BELLA (BERTONE) Geneva, March **1999**. Front-engine two-seater coupé based on the Alfa Romeo 166 and having a very intimate treatment of the cockpit. Engine: 3-litre V6. Power: 230bhp. Length: 445cm. Width: 189.5cm. Height: 131cm. Wheelbase: 270cm.

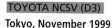

To celebrate its 70th anniversary, which coincided with the year 2000, Pininfarina linked its name once more with Ferrari to create a new dream roadster.

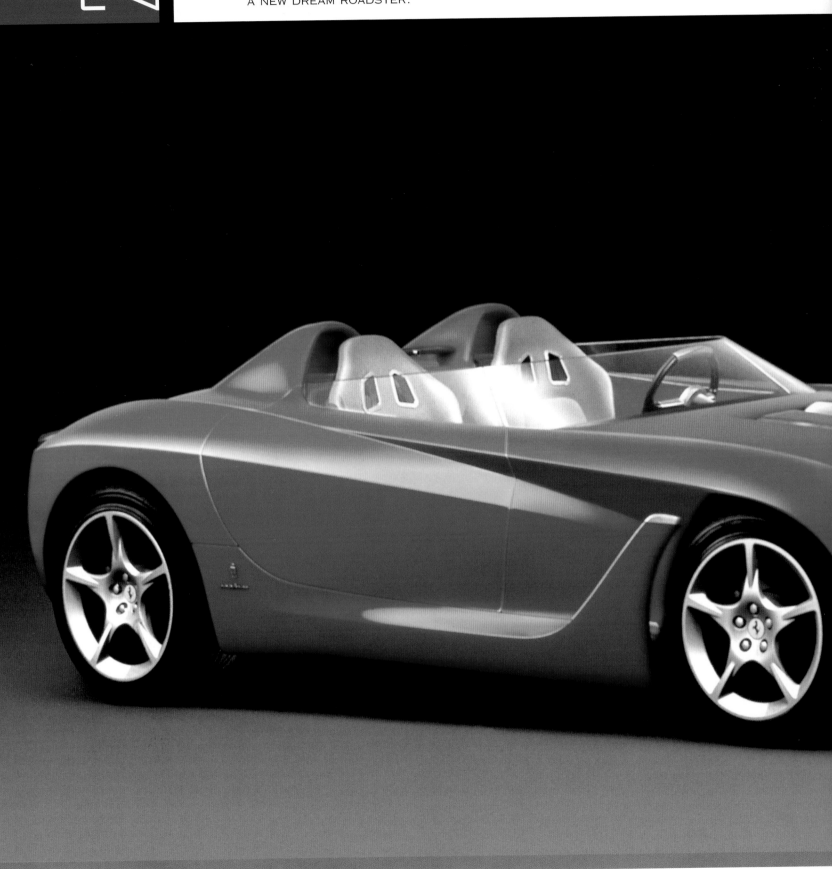

FERRARI ROSSA (PININFARINA)

Turin, June 2000. The Pininfarina enterprise was founded in 1930 by Battista 'Pinin' Farina. The emblematic year 2000 was thus the occasion for the Turin firm to celebrate its 70th birthday with a bang. The choice of a symbolic marque came completely naturally: it fell on Ferrari, whose privileged partner Pininfarina has been since 1952.

For such an anniversary the *Studi e Ricerche* department, run by Lorenzo Ramaciotti, set out an ambitious brief. Pininfarina chose to make a true 'dream car'. It was to be a thoroughly sporting *barchetta*, with a front engine, using the mechanicals of the Ferrari 550 Maranello. The glazing, limited to a cowl, swept completely around the cockpit and the headrests were extended into tail fairings.

The style bore the signature of Ken Okuyama, a highly talented designer who already had the Peugeot Nautilus to his credit and who would be responsible for other important designs such as the Ferrari FX and the future Maserati *Quattroporte* before leaving Pininfarina.

In the Rossa there was something of the Mythos, although that was a car built around a mid-mounted engine. The sculptural working of the sides, the wingline that emphasised the cockpit, the plump back end like the hind-quarters of a carthorse and the game of contrasts between concave and convex surfaces all recalled the Mythos – as well as the general proportions with the long nose and the short rear overhang. Finishing off the effect, a gulping cross-hatched grille gobbled at the tarmac.

Behind the front wheels the side panels were hollowed out in the fashion of the 1958 Testa Rossa. That said, the project was not burdened with sterile references to the past. A vertical spar, floating free like an aircraft tail-fin, its edge following the curve of the wheel, swept the wingline along the length of the sills.

The Rossa was powered by a V12 engine of 5,474cc, developing 485bhp. It retained the Maranello wheelbase of 250cm, but its dimensions were more compact, with a length of 429cm, a width of 194cm and a 113cm height.

The Japanese stylist Ken Okuyama concocted this complex exercise to celebrate Pininfarina's 70th birthday. It was based on the mechanics of the Ferrari 550 Maranello.

SEAT SALSA EMOCION

PEUGEOT FÉLINE

PEUGEOT FÉLINE **Geneva, March 2000**. Two-seater front-engined coupé-cabrio; carbon-fibre monocoque. At the Paris show Peugeot would show the City Toyz (Vroomaster, Kart up, Bobslid and e-doll) and – heralding the 307 – the Prométhée. Engine: 2,946cc V6. Power: 210bhp. Length: 407cm. Width: 188cm. Height: 119cm. Wheelbase: 258cm.

SEAT SALSA EMOCION **Paris, September 2000**. Off-road MPV, derived from Salsa concept car (Geneva 2000). The MDS ('Multi Driving Concept') system allowed ground clearance to be varied. Four-wheel drive; Tiptronic transmission. Engine: 2.8-litre transverse V6. Power: 250bhp at 6,200rpm. Maximum torque: 219lb ft at 3,200rpm. Length: 416.2cm. Width: 188.6cm. Height: 159.3cm. Wheelbase: 259.1cm. Maximum speed: 145mph.

JEEP VARSITY **Detroit, January 2000**. Four-door two-box off-road saloon. Engine: 3.5-litre V6. Power: 300bhp. Other concept cars shown at Detroit included the Buick LaCrosse, Chevrolet SSR, Chrysler 300 Hemi C, Dodge Maxxcab, Ford Prodigy and Equator, General Motors Precept, GMC Terradyne, Hummer H2, Jaguar F-type, Mercedes-Benz Vision SLA, Mitsubishi SSR, Oldsmobile Profile, Saturn CV-1 and Volkswagen AAC.

RENAULT KOLEOS

JEEP VARSITY

CITROËN OSMOSE (D3)

RENAULT KOLEOS **Geneva, March 2000**. Innovatory concept for an off-road MPV, hybrid-powered using a 16v 2-litre turbo engine driving the front wheels and an electric motor driving the rear wheels. Variable-height suspension; 21in wheels. Length: 451cm. Width: 190cm. Height: 160cm/170cm. Wheelbase: 274cm.

FORD 24.7

MASERATI BURAN (ITALDESIGN-GIUGIARO)

FORD 24.7 **Detroit, January 2000**. Concept taking in a series of communications and telemetry technologies developed by Visteon Automotive Systems. Designed with a stripped-down simplicity under the direction of J Mays, head of Ford design since 1998. Built on Focus platform lengthened by 5cm, and proposed as an estate, a pick-up or a coupé. Engine: Zetec 2-litre 4-cyl. At the 1999 Tokyo show Ford had shown the similarly-inspired 021C of Mark Newson.

CITROËN OSMOSE (D3) **Paris, September 2000**. A symbol of conviviality, exploring the interchangeability of status between pedestrian and motorist. First concept car developed under Jean-Pierre Ploué after his 1999 arrival at Citroën; built by D3; Height: 170cm.

AUDI STEPPENWOLF

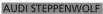

MASERATI BURAN (ITALDESIGN-GIUGIARO)

MASERATI BURAN (ITALDESIGN-GIUGIARO) **Turin, June 2000**. Grand-touring 4wd 'monospace' built by IDC, Italdesign's new Californian offshoot. Engine: 3.2-litre turbo V8. Power: 370bhp. Length: 498.3cm. Width: 195cm. Height: 163cm. Wheelbase: 293cm.

AUDI STEPPENWOLF **Paris, September 2000**. Off-road coupé with variable (16.3cm to 22.3cm) ground clearance, thanks to its pneumatic suspension. Engine: 3.2-litre V6. Power: 225bhp. Length: 421cm. Width: 183cm. Height: 146cm. Maximum speed: 143mph.

ISUZU ZEN

MITSUBISHI SPACELINER (MIM)

ISUZU ZEN Tokyo, **October 2001**. Vehicle combining the appointments of a 4x4 with the functionality of a delivery van. Created by ITCE-Design under Atsuhiko Yamada; designer Geoffrey Gardiner. The side windows evoked a fan and the interior converted into an area similar to a Japanese tearoom, with a floor covered in rush matting. Engine: 3-litre dohc 24v V6. Automatic transmission. Length: 448cm. Width: 190cm. Height: 198cm. Wheelbase: 305cm.

CITROËN C-CROSSER (D3) Frankfurt, September **2001**. Leisure off-roader featuring a folding glass roof and drive-by-wire controls allowing the steering wheel to be moved across the width of the car; designed under Jean-Pierre Ploué. Automatic transmission, 4wd, ESP, Hydractive suspension. Engine: 2-litre HPI 4-cyl.

CADILLAC VIZON

CITROËN C-CROSSER (D3)

CITROËN OSÉE (PININFARINA)

CITROËN OSÉE (PININFARINA) Geneva, March **2001**. Mid-engined GT designed by Nicolas Jardin, under Lorenzo Ramaciotti. Engine: 2,946cc V6. Power: 194bhp. Five-speed automatic gearbox. Length: 415cm. Width: 189.5cm. Height: 115.6cm. Wheelbase: 265cm.

MITSUBISHI SPACELINER (MIM) Tokyo, October 2001. This elegant 4wd *grande routière* symbolised the arrival at Mitsubishi of Olivier Boulay, who had left Daimler-Chrysler in May 2001. In a reference to Japanese traditions, the carpet suggested a Zen garden! Alongside it at Tokyo Mitsubishi showed the S.U.P., CZ-2 and CZ-3 Tarmac concept cars. Length: 490cm. Width: 188cm. Height: 153cm. Wheelbase: 295cm.

CADILLAC VIZON Detroit, January 2001. An evolution of the Sports Utility Vehicle towards a sporting estate; design directed by Tom Kearns. Engine: 4.2-litre Northstar V8. Length: 486.2cm. Width: 180cm. Height: 163cm. Wheelbase: 304.8cm

SAAB 9X Frankfurt, September 2001. This 4wd coupé with an estate flavour marked the arrival at Saab of Michael Mauer, to be in charge of design, and Anthony Lo as head of advanced design. Engine: 3-litre 24v V6. Power: 300bhp. Length: 415.6cm. Width: 182cm. Height: 136.5cm. Maximum speed: 150mph. 0–60mph: 5.9 seconds.

SAAB 9X

RENAULT TALISMAN

RENAULT TALISMAN Frankfurt, September 2001. Four-seater coupé with flat fixed seats and adjustable dashboard. Wide gullwing doors operated by card. Designed by Stéphane Janin under Michel Jardin, directed by Patrick Le Quément. Engine: 4.5-litre 32v Nissan V8, longitudinally mounted. Automatic gearbox. Length: 480.5cm. Width: 195cm. Height: 138cm. Wheelbase: 295cm. Weight: 1,600kg.

MAZDA MX SPORT TOURER Geneva, March 2001. Successor to the Nextourer (Frankfurt and Tokyo 1999); mix of estate and coupé, with tailgate opening downwards. Hybrid power: 2-litre 4-cyl engine and 40kW electric motor. Length: 457.5cm. Width: 179cm. Height: 143cm. Wheelbase: 267cm.

MAZDA MX SPORT TOURER

2002

ONCE AGAIN, ALFA ROMEO MECHANICALS INSPIRED A SUPERB CONCEPT CAR.
SUBLIMATED BY THE MAGIC OF THE MILANESE MARQUE, THE ART OF GIORGIO
GIUGIARO WAS TRULY AT ITS APOGEE.

Geneva, **March 2002**. The history of car design has always wavered between two temptations. As in all sectors of creative work, automotive coachwork has always been prey to two major trends: the conservative current of thought, burdened with historical references and extolling mannerism and old-school elitist luxury, and the progressive current of thought, nourished by modernity, stipulating a certain purity, and singing the praises of standardised production.

Giorgio Giugiaro has defended and illustrated both these facets of the creative process throughout his career. Capable of proposing novel concepts such as the Fiat Panda, the Capsula and the Megagamma, Giugiaro has counterbalanced this tendency by putting his name to some genuinely splendid coachwork in the great traditions of the past. The Alfa Romeo Brera, styled by the maestro in person, belongs in this prodigious sequence.

The car responds to traditional canons of aesthetics, with its ideal proportions playing on the contrast between the long bonnet, the abbreviated rear and the flat-roofed set-back cockpit. The treatment of the volumes is sober, and uses the

ALFA ROMEO BRERA (ITALDESIGN)

The Brera brought together the key elements for a landmark vehicle: a strong style with references to the culture of the marque in question, and an aristocratic set of mechanicals.

most classical of detailing: muscular wheelarches and a shouldered waistline. This front-engined GT is a realistic proposition, and was created with a view to series production, according to Giugiaro.

The Bera has an Alfa Romeo V8 of Ferrari origin, mated to a six-speed sequential gearbox. It is 438.8cm long, 189.4cm wide and 128.9cm high, and is built on a 259.5cm wheelbase.

ROVER TCV

PEUGEOT RC PIQUE/CARREAU

PEUGEOT RC PIQUE/CARREAU **Geneva, March 2002**. Mid-engined 2+2 coupé designed by Nicolas Brissonneau under Gérard Welter. Two variants: petrol-engined (1,997cc and 180bhp) Pique and turbo-diesel (2,168cc and 175bhp) Carreau. Wheelbase: 280cm. Weight: 900–950kg. Maximum speed: 143mph.

CADILLAC CIEN

CADILLAC CIEN
Detroit, January 2002. Mid-engined GT with carbon-fibre body and chassis, created to celebrate Cadillac's 100th birthday. Engine: 7.5-litre Northstar XV12. Power: 750bhp. Gearbox: 6-sp semi-automatic. Length: 445.7cm. Width: 197.5cm. Height: 117cm. Wheelbase: 275cm.

NISSAN YANYA
Geneva, March 2002. Basic 4wd vehicle ('E-4WD' transmission) with rear wheels driven by electric motors. Four separate seats and full-length opening roof.

ROVER TCV **Geneva, March 2002**. Sporting estate ('Tourer Concept Vehicle') which marked the arrival of Peter Stevens as head of Rover design. Based on a shortened Rover 75 platform.

GM AUTONOMY **Detroit, January 2002**. Futurist vehicle featuring hydrogen propulsion and an engine powered by a fuel cell (GAPC). Length: 436.5cm. Width: 188cm. Height: 124.7cm. Wheelbase: 309.9cm.

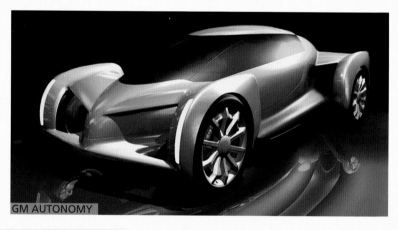

GM AUTONOMY

NISSAN YANYA

SAAB NOVANTA (BERTONE) **Geneva, March 2002**. Saloon based on Saab 9-5, built to celebrate Bertone's 90th anniversary. Designed under Giuliano Biasio, in charge of exterior style since 1999. Drive-by-wire controls. Engine: 3-litre 24v V6. Power: 200bhp at 5,000rpm. Maximum torque: 229lb ft at 2,200rpm. Length: 445cm. Width: 180cm. Height: 145cm.

VOLKSWAGEN MAGELLAN

FIORAVANTI YAK (CECOMP)

VOLKSWAGEN MAGELLAN **Detroit, January 2002**. Luxury off-roader created by Volkswagen's Design Centre Europe at Sitges in Spain. Engine: W8. Power: 275bhp. Length: 468.5cm. Width: 186cm. Height: 162cm.

FIORAVANTI YAK (CECOMP) **Geneva, March 2002**. Leisure off-roader. Original side-panel treatment; lateral windscreen-wipers. Engine: V8. Length: 450cm. Width: 191cm. Height: 168cm. Wheelbase: 280cm.

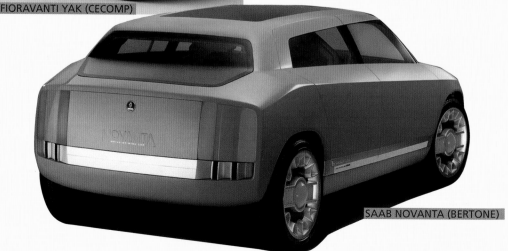

SAAB NOVANTA (BERTONE)

Model	Year	Page
MATRA P29	1986	92
MATRA M25 (D3)	1989	97
MAZDA RX-500	1970	60
MAZDA MX-81 (BERTONE)	1981	81
MAZDA MX-03	1985	89
MAZDA MX SPORT TOURER	2001	121
MAYBACH ZEPPELIN DS8 (SPOHN)	1932	12
MAYBACH SW 35 STROMLINIE (SPOHN)	1935	13
MERCEDES-BENZ 170H (AVA)	1939	16
MERCEDES-BENZ 230 SL SPÉCIALE (PININFARINA)	1964	48
MERCEDES-BENZ C111	1969	57
MERCEDES-BENZ ESF 13	1972	64
MERCEDES-BENZ F200 IMAGINATION (STOLA)	1996	112
MERCER COBRA (SIBONA-BASANO)	1964	48
MERCURY XM-800	1954	28
MERCURY PALOMAR	1962	44
MERCURY AURORA	1964	48
MERCURY MC4	1997	113
MG EX-E	1985	89
MITSUBISHI MP90X	1985	89
MITSUBISHI HSR	1987	93
MITSUBISHI SPACELINER (MIM)	2001	121

N

Model	Year	Page
NISSAN 126 X	1970	60
NISSAN 216 X	1971	61
NISSAN CUE-X	1985	89
NISSAN ARC-X	1987	93
NISSAN TRI-X	1991	101
NISSAN AP-X	1993	105
NISSAN YANYA	2002	124
NORTH-LUCAS	1922	8
NSU TRAPÈZE	1973	65
NSU Ro80 (GMARMEIER)	1975	69

O

Model	Year	Page
OLDSMOBILE 88 CUTLASS	1954	28
OLDSMOBILE GOLDEN ROCKET	1957	33
OLDSMOBILE AEROTECH	1986	92
OLDSMOBILE INCAS (ITAL DESIGN)	1986	92
OLDSMOBILE EXPRESSION	1990	100
OPEL RAK 2	1929	9
OPEL GT-2 (MICHELOTTI)	1975	69
OPEL JUNIOR	1983	85
OPELCHRONOS (PININFARINA)	1991	101
OPEL TWIN	1992	104
OPEL MAXX	1995	109
OPEL SLALOM (BERTONE)	1996	112

P

Model	Year	Page
PACKARD PAN AMERICAN	1952	24
PACKARD PANTHER DAYTONA	1954	28
PANHARD DYNAVIA	1948	18-19
PEERLESS XD	1931	12
PEGASO Z-102 (EL DOMINICANO)	1952	24
PEGASO Z-102 THRILL (TOURING)	1953	25
PERSU AUTOMOBIL AERODYNAMIC	1923	8
PEUGEOT 402 N4X '1940'	1936	14-15
PEUGEOT TAXI H4 (HEULIEZ)	1972	64
PEUGEOT PEUGETTE (PININFARINA)	1976	72
PEUGEOT QUASAR	1984	86-87
PEUGEOT PROXIMA	1986	92
PEUGEOT OXIA	1988	94-95

Model	Year	Page
PEUGEOT ION	1994	108
PEUGEOT ASPHALTE	1996	112
PEUGEOT FÉLINE	2000	120
PEUGEOT RC PIQUE/CARREAU	2002	124
PHANTOM CORSAIR (BOHMANN & SCHWARTZ)	1938	16
PIERCE ARROW SILVER ARROW	1933	12
PININFARINA ETHOS	1992	104
PININFARINA ETHOS 3	1994	108
PININFARINA METROCUBO	1999	117
PFX (PININ FARINA)	1960	40
PFY (PININFARINA)	1961	41
PF SIGMA (PININFARINA)	1963	45
PLYMOUTH ASSIMETRICA (GHIA)	1961	41
PLYMOUTH SLINGSHOT	1988	96
PORSCHE 911 ROADSTER (BERTONE)	1966	52
PORSCHE KARISMA (BERTONE)	1994	108
PONTIAC CLUB DE MER	1956	32
PONTIAC BANSHEE	1966	52
PONTIAC BANSHEE II	1976	72
PONTIAC TYPE K	1977	73
PONTIAC TRANS SPORT	1986	92
PONTIAC PURSUIT	1987	93
PONTIAC STINGER	1989	97
PONTIAC SUNFIRE	1990	100
PONTIAC PROTOSPORT4	1991	101
PSA TULIP	1995	109

R

Model	Year	Page
RENAULT JUVAQUATRE TAXI (FAGET-VARNET)	1945	17
RENAULT JUVAQUATRE TAXI	1949	20
RENAULT 4 CV VUTOTAL (LABOURDETTE)	1950	21
RENAULT 8 COUPÉ (GHIA)	1964	48
RENAULT BRV	1974	68
RENAULT EVE	1980	80
RENAULT VESTA	1982	84
RENAULT GABBIANO (ITAL DESIGN)	1983	85
RENAULT MÉGANE (G-STUDIO)	1988	96
RENAULT LAGUNA (D3)	1990	98-99
RENAULT SCÉNIC	1991	101
RENAULT ZOOM (MATRA)	1992	104
RENAULT RACOON	1993	105
RENAULT ESPACE F1 (MATRA)	1994	106-107
RENAULT ARGOS	1994	108
RENAULT INITIALE (G-STUDIO)	1995	109
RENAULT FIFTIE (D3)	1996	112
RENAULT VEL SATIS	1998	116
RENAULT KOLEOS	2000	120
RENAULT TALISMAN (G-STUDIO)	2001	121
ROVER JET 1	1950	21
ROVER T3	1956	32
ROVER P6BS/LEYLAND EIGHT	1968	56
ROVER MINI SPIRITUAL/MINI SPIRITUAL TWO	1997	113
ROVER MINI ACV30	1997	113
ROVER TCV	2002	124

S

Model	Year	Page
SAAB VIKING (RAYTON FISSORE)	1982	84
SAAB EV-1	1985	89
SAAB 9X	2001	121
SAAB NOVANTA (BERTONE)	2002	124
SBARRO STASH PIERRE CARDIN	1975	69
SBARRO ROYALE	1979	77
SBARRO SUPER TWELVE	1982	84

Model	Year	Page
SBARRO CHALLENGE	1985	89
SEAT SALSA EMOCION	2000	120
SELENE (GHIA)	1959	37
STAR JET (VIGNALE)	1963	45
SOCÉMA-GRÉGOIRE	1952	22-23
SCIMITAR HARDTOP CONVERTIBLE (REUTTER)	1959	37
SENSAUD DE LAVAUD 17 HP	1927	9
SERENISSIMA (GHIA)	1968	56
SIMCA FULGUR	1959	37
STANGUELLINI 1200 SPIDER (BERTONE)	1957	33
STOUT SCARAB	1935	13
SUBARU SAGRES	1993	105
SUZUKI RT-1	1987	93
SUZUKI CONSTELLATION	1989	97

T

Model	Year	Page
TALBOT STAR SIX	1959	37
TASCO	1949	20
TOYOTA EX-III	1969	57
TOYOTA EX-7	1970	60
TOYOTA RV-2	1972	64
TOYOTA MP-1	1975	69
TOYOTA ABEV	1977	73
TOYOTA CX-80	1979	77
TOYOTA FX-1	1983	85
TOYOTA GTV	1987	93
TOYOTA NCSV (D3)	1999	117
TRIUMPH TR3 COUPÉ (VIGNALE)	1958	36

V

Model	Year	Page
VAUXHALL XVR	1966	52
VAUXHALL SRV	1970	60
VAUXHALL EQUUS	1978	76
VOISIN 'VOITURE DE L'AVENIR'	1934	13
VOISIN BISCOOTER	1950	21
VOLANIS HÉLIOS	1983	85
VOLANIS APOLLON	1984	88
VOLKSWAGEN STUDENT	1984	88
VOLKSWAGEN SCOOTER	1986	92
VOLKSWAGEN MAGELLAN	2002	124
VOLVO VENUS BILO (NORDBERGS)	1933	12
VOLVO TUNDRA (BERTONE)	1979	77
VOLVO LCP2000	1983	85
VW-PORSCHE MURÈNE (HEULIEZ)	1970	60
VW-PORSCHE TAPIRO (ITAL DESIGN)	1970	60

W

Model	Year	Page
WIMILLE FORD (FAGET-VARNET)	1948	20
WIMILLE FORD (FAGET-VARNET)	1950	21

Z

Model	Year	Page
ZENDER VISION 3	1987	93

Contents

Photographic credits: Personal collection of S. Bellu.